Doris Lessing: A Life Behind the Scenes

PETER LANG
PROMPT

PETER LANG

Oxford • Bern • Berlin • Bruxelles • New York • Wien

Peter Raina

Doris Lessing: A Life Behind the Scenes

The Files of the British Intelligence Service MI5

PETER LANG

Oxford • Bern • Berlin • Bruxelles • New York • Wien

Bibliographic information published by **Die Deutsche Nationalbibliothek.**
Die Deutsche Nationalbibliothek lists this publication in the "Deutsche
Nationalbibliografie"; detailed bibliographic data are available
on the Internet at http://dnb.d-nb.de/.

A catalogue record for this book is available from the British Library.

Library of Congress Control Number: 2021006416

A CIP catalog record for this book has been applied for at the Library of Congress.

ISBN 978-1-80079-183-1 (print) • ISBN 978-1-80079-184-8 (ePDF)
ISBN 978-1-80079-185-5 (ePub) • ISBN 978-1-80079-186-2 (mobi)

© Peter Lang Group AG 2021
Published by Peter Lang Ltd, International Academic Publishers, 52 St Giles,
Oxford, OX1 3LU, United Kingdom
oxford@peterlang.com, www.peterlang.com

This publication has been peer reviewed.

Doris Lessing with her son, Peter

To
Janice, Manju, Suren, Lalit, Ashni
with affection

CONTENTS

LIST OF ILLUSTRATIONS

Frontispiece

Doris Lessing with her son, Peter. By courtesy of Gabriele
Gysi, Berlin (private collection).   v

Within the book

All these photographs were made accessible to the author by
Mrs Gabriele Gysi (Berlin) from her private collection. Frau
Gabriele is the daughter of Irene Gysi, sister of Gottfried Lessing.

Preface

This small volume is not a study in biography, nor is it a treatise on the literary qualities of a very distinguished British novelist. Its designs are more modest. It presents reports of the British security service, MI5, recording the activities of Doris Lessing, especially while she was a member of the British Communist Party from 1952 until 1956. Doris never made a secret of her sympathies for communism, but openly proclaimed them. She helped in founding communist cells; she played an active role in the Soviet-sponsored peace movement; she travelled to the Soviet Union with other left-wing intellectuals and, on her return, highly commended the achievements of communism in that country, doing so in several public lectures. Doris had come to hold communist views while she was still residing in Southern Rhodesia, mainly because she deplored the colour bar imposed by the white colonials so strongly. She found the unjust social status forced upon the natives utterly abhorrent, and since the imperial rulers showed no desire to remedy the atrocious conditions of the Africans, she earnestly believed that the road to freedom lay in communism.

While she remained in Southern Rhodesia, Doris was not a principal player. Her enthusiasm for the cause had her distributing left-wing literature and little more. It was only when she arrived in Britain in 1949 that she adopted more purposeful measures to further Marxist objectives. She attended communist meetings, borrowed books from the Left Wing Book Club and developed contact with various comrades. She became a full member of the British Communist Party in 1952, and from that moment on, she was a suspicious person so far as the British security service MI5 was concerned. And this is where our story begins.

Her telephone was bugged, her correspondence intercepted[1] and her meetings were closely documented by the agency. Although it was against the law, MI5 continued to keep a close eye on her. Whenever Doris Lessing

---

1   This system had been in practice since 1911 under a Home Office Warrant (HOW) authorizing the examination of all the correspondence of particular people upon a

visited Southern Rhodesia. the local security service documented all her spheres of action, and sent reports to MI5. These reports were not available until recently. We publish them here for the first time.

What do they tell us?

First, they show how the security service employed what they called 'well-placed sources' to gather information: and how that information was secured.

Secondly, we learn about Doris's movements and her whereabouts in London, the people she met, what meetings she attended and what she said.

Thirdly, the security services were chiefly interested in what Lessing did when she visited Southern Rhodesia. There she met all the important African trade unionists and political activists. She advised them on how to coordinate their work towards the achievement of their aim of securing release from oppression. She advised them (and this we must emphasize) that all their activities must be peaceful, never volatile or violently revolutionary. She recommended that Africans showing promise should be sent to Britain for further education. The South African security service reported all her activities in Africa and forwarded these reports to the British security service, so that we have records about Doris from Rhodesia as well as from Britain.

We also know from the MI5 files that Doris Lessing never received any instructions from the Soviet Secret Service. Whatever she did, whoever she met and wherever she went, it was all on her own initiative. The British Secret Service records tell us what exactly Doris attempted to achieve as a communist. This information, unknown before, reveals a life behind the scenes (hence our title), which should be indispensable to any future Lessing biographer.

In 1956, when Stalin's crimes became public and when Soviet troops invaded Hungary, Doris left the British Communist Party and her ambition to change the dismal life circumstances of Africans through communism totally disappeared. Years later she explained why. The underlying problem, she said, was the way Party members maltreated the language: how words were misused:

---

list. A standard work on the history of Rhodesia is that by Robert Blake, *A History of Rhodesia* (London: Eyre Methuen, 1977).

It is not a new thought that communism debased language and with language, thought. There is a communist jargon recognizable after a single sentence. [...] Even five or six years ago *Izvestia*, *Pravda*, and a thousand other communist papers were written in a language that seemed designed to fill up as much space as possible without actually saying anything – because, of course, it was dangerous to take up positions that might have to be defended.[2]

With language unable to reflect on reality and ask hard questions, it was 'possible to divorce oneself from life or to *live in an ivory tower*'. And what had happened?

The writers who were to write about social injustice, took power in 1917. It became socialist realism. Anyone who had the misfortune to read through a lot of that stuff, which I did in London early in the '50s for a communist publisher, knows that socialist realism created novels written in a language as dead as the books already mentioned as a product of academia. Why? Writers know instinctively that a recipe for writing dead books is to write because you ought.[3]

Despotism was 'an evident child of Communism'. How wrong it was, Doris came to think, that:

our minds have been set by Communism [... The] left wing, the social, even liberal movements of Europe have been terminally damaged because the progressive imagination was captured by the Soviet experience. The Russian Revolution, the Soviet Union, was a paradigm, whether seen as a success or as a failed experiment which could have been better. For decades, for half a century, for three-quarters of a century, all the *tender-hearted* people longing for better things were preoccupied with the Soviet Union, with its history of murder, mass murder, show trials. A history, and this I'm sure is the important thing in the long run, of failure.[4]

And how equally frustrating it was that the entire

progressive movement of Europe has had its imagination in thrall to the Soviet experience, an experience in fact irrelevant to Europe. It would be easily possible to

---

2   See Doris Lessing in conversation: Edith Kurzweil, 'Unexamined Mental Attitudes Left Behind by Communism', in Earl G. Ingersoll (Ed.), *Doris Lessing: Conversations* (Princeton, New Jersey: Ontario Review Press, 1994), 204.
3   *Ibid.*, 206.
4   *Ibid.*, 211.

make an alternative reality, a history of Europe that had made a decision to develop socialism, or even a just society, without any reference at all to the Soviet Union. [...] We did not have to identify with the Soviet Union, with its seventy-odd years of logic-chopping, of idiotic rhetoric, brutality, concentration camps, pogroms against the Jews. Again and again, failure.[5]

The history of the Soviet Union, Doris came to conclude, has been 'a tragedy, for the Russians and the other communist nations now free'.

Doris would never 'have anything to do with politics again' unless she 'was forced at the point of a gun'.[6] She was basically a writer and would occupy herself with the relationship between the individual and political groups and with the problems that continually arise between men and women.

This present volume, *Doris Lessing: A Life Behind the Scenes*, has three main sections. The first provides a background. It explains why Doris embraced communist ideology in the first place, briefly describes the British Communist Party, and offers a short account of MI5, the British security service from whom our files are drawn. The second section presents the secret files kept on Doris Lessing from the 1940s to the very early '60s. They record Doris's activities while she was active as a communist. Surveillance waned and then stopped when Doris resigned from the Party in the wake of the events of 1956. She then devoted her talents to writing. As she insisted, she had come to Britain principally with the intention 'to earn my living by writing'. And she did indeed become a great writer. She wrote both fiction and non-fiction with great persuasive and imaginative power. Though these writings are outside the scope of the present study, a third section is added, as an epilogue, pointing out some especially remarkable features to be found in them, and there is also a brief bibliography.

PETER RAINA
Christmas 2020
Berlin

5   *Ibid.*, 212.
6   See Christopher Bigsby, 'The Need to Tell Stories', in Earl G. Ingersoll (Ed.), *Doris Lessing: Conversations*, 74.

Acknowledgements

I am chiefly indebted to The National Archives, Kew, Richmond, Surrey for granting me access to the British Security Service Personal Files: Communists and Suspected Communists, Including Russian and Communist Sympathisers: *Doris May Lessing*. This material is a Crown Copyright public record, reproduced in this volume under the terms of the *Open Government Licence* (OGL). (*Reference*: Public sector information enquiry – Ref: TNA1606756048B61: e-mail dated 01.12.2020 from Judy Nokes, Copyright, Crown Copyright and Information Policy Adviser, The National Archives, Kew, Richmond, Surrey.)

I also tender my gratitude to:
Jon Ashby, copy-editor, Winchester
Mrs Gabriele Gysi, Berlin
Mrs Halina Kolodziejczyk-Raina, Berlin
Mrs Lucy Melville, Publishing Director, Peter Lang Ltd., Oxford
Dr Marek Pottle, Isaiah Berlin Legacy Fellow, Wolfson College, Oxford

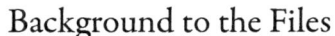

Background to the Files

Why Doris Lessing Became a Communist

People become communists, Doris Lessing wrote in her memoirs:

> because of cynicism about their own governments – that, first. Because they had fallen
> in love with a Communist – as Gottfried Lessing did. Because they were taken to a Party
> rally and were swept away by mass emotion. Because they had been taken to a Party
> meeting and found the atmosphere of conspiracy appealing. Because of the idealism
> of the Party. Because they had a taste for heroics or suffering. In my case it was because
> for the first time in my life I was meeting a group of people (not an isolated individual
> here and there), who read everything, and who did not think it remarkable to read,
> and among whom thoughts about the Native Problem I had scarcely dared to say aloud
> turned out to be mere commonplace. I became a Communist because of the spirit of
> the times, because of the *Zeitgeist*.[1]

A report by MI6 underlines this confession: 'Her communist sympathies
have been fanned almost to the point of fanaticism owing to her upbringing
in Rhodesia, which has brought out in her a deep hatred of the colour bar.
Colonial exploitation is her pet theme and she has now nearly become as irresponsible in her statements as COPPARD saying that everything black is
wonderful and that all men and all things white are vicious.'[2]

There is one further reason why Doris decided to become a communist,
however, and that was that it gave her the sexual freedom she craved – a
desire to be promiscuous. 'There have been times in my life,' she confessed,
when 'I have been obsessed with sex.' She left her first husband, Frank
Wisdom,[3] not because he was a civil servant and thus a 'reactionary', but

---

1   Doris Lessing, *Under My Skin: Volume One of My Autobiography, to 1949*
     (London: Flamingo, 1995), 259.
2   MI6 Report 97, 471, 29 September 1952. The 'Coppard' reference is to the short story
     writer A. E. Coppard, who was one of Doris's associates with Soviet sympathies.
3   Doris married Frank Charles Wisdom in 1937. Frank, a civil servant in the Southern
     Rhodesian government, was born on 6 September 1910 in Midlands Rhodesia.
     He died on 11 June 1981. Doris was born as Doris Taylor on 22 October 1919 in
     Kermanshah (Persia) of British parents. Her father, Alfred, was then an employee of
     the Imperial Bank of Persia. The Taylor family returned to England in 1924, but in

because she longed for unrestricted sexual relations: 'I wanted to live differently,' Doris relates. 'In fact, I was having a love affair. Rather, an affair. I was not in love with him nor he with me, but it was the spirit of the times.'[4] Doris divorced her second husband, Gottfried Lessing,[5] for the same reason. 'We had never intended to stay married,' she writes. 'We had been forced into marriage by circumstances.'[6] But they had a son, Peter, born in 1947. Then she had met another communist, an Afrikaans artist. 'The love affair was only possible because of my naivety. [...] I went off with this artist [...] in his car, to where we sat on the high slopes above

---

1925 moved to the British colony of Southern Rhodesia to farm maize on 400 hectares of bushland. In 1937 Doris obtained a job as a telephone operator in Salisbury, where she met Frank Wisdom. She was just 18 years old, and Frank nine years older. She married because she had become pregnant. 'I was not in love with him,' Doris explained later, 'though such were the intoxications of the time it was easy to think so. He was not in love with me. [...] we were both rational, and un-religious, perhaps I should say anti-religious.' See Doris Lessing, *Under My Skin*, 206–7. Frank was often 'sulky, sometimes for days, angry, self-pitying, full of reproaches, and always about things we both knew were off the point. Meanwhile I was bright, false, *reasonable* – hypocritical. [...] He was drinking a lot. Nothing new about that. [...] we all drank [...]'. *Ibid.*, 237. They had two children. The marriage ended in 1943.

4   Doris Lessing, *Under My Skin*, 265.

5   Doris married Gottfried Anton Nicolai Lessing in 1943. Gottfried had had a chequered life. He was born to German-Jewish parents on 14 December 1914 in St Petersburg, where his father worked as a mining Engineer in Tsarist Russia. With the outbreak of World War I, the Lessings were expelled from Russia because they were Germans, and returned to Berlin. Gottfried attended secondary school (*Gymnasium*) there from 1928 to 1933, and then studied jurisprudence and economy at the University of Berlin. Afterwards he went to Hamburg to work in a law firm, and in 1937 took a doctorate in Jurisprudence in that city. Being part-Jewish, Gottfried had to leave Nazi Germany at the beginning of 1938. He first went to Great Britain, where he joined The London Assurance as an unpaid clerk, but in 1939 migrated to Rhodesia to work in the overseas branch of a London insurance company. Up to 1941 he also worked as a casual labourer in various places. He eventually found a job in a solicitor's office, where he could resume work as a lawyer. In 1942 Gottfried became one of the founders of the Rhodesian Communist Party, and was later its president. It was at one of the Party meetings that Gottfried got to know Doris.

6   *Lessing, Under My Skin*, 347.

Cape Town and watched cloud pour over an edge of hills like milk into a dish. We necked. With much pleasure and promise.'[7] Thus Doris 'ditched' one husband after another, 'but all's fair in love.'[8]

Doris was a communist 'perhaps for two years, in Southern Rhodesia, from 1942 to 1944'.[9] This was in Salisbury after she had met in 'the street Dorothy Schwartz, that dissident member of the group of *progressives* who long ago (but it was four years) had thought me a suitable recruit'. Dorothy thought that Doris should come along to a meeting of these progressives, making it clear that she did not 'mean those stupid social democrats'; rather, they were 'a group of real revolutionaries and they thought it was time they met me. This kind of flattery is hard to withstand.'[10] Subsequently Doris visited the local Left Book Club frequently, spending time with 'the comrades every evening and some part of every day':[11] 'We were at every kind of meeting, study group, seminar, or engaged in starting yet another organization, for it seemed that almost at once there were at least a dozen. Medical Aid for Russia, as it sounds, was to get money and pay for medical and other supplies for our gallant ally.'[12] Other activities included the sale of communist literature.

Why did she get engaged in these activities? Or, in her own words, 'What were the ideas that fuelled us?' She herself supplies an answer. She believed:

> First, that, within ten years, well fifteen, the whole world would be Communist, from free choice, because of the manifest superiorities of Communism. There would be no race prejudice, oppression of women, exploitation of labour – no snobbishness or contempt of others. The paradise would follow a brief period of resistance by reactionaries, only a minority, after all, because by then 'the State would have withered away'. This phrase, 'the withering away of the State', together with 'the contradictions of capitalism', were by far the most common sources of the sardonic jokes with which the comrades everywhere indicated they were not lost to sanity.

7   *Ibid.*, 353.
8   *Ibid.*, 353.
9   *Ibid.*, 275.
10 *Ibid.*, 258.
11 *Ibid.*, 261.
12 *Ibid.*, 270.

Paradise, then, was the world's agenda, and soon. Who would lead the world thither? Why, we would, people like us, Communists, the vanguard of the working class, destined by History for the role. [...]

Secondly, there was no way to paradise but by Revolution. [...] It was morally superior to believe in Revolution, and those who did not were at the least, cowardly. [...]

Thirdly, we were a part of a family that covered the world. [...]

Fourthly, a Communist should always be better than everyone else: work harder, study more, look after people, always be ready to do the dirty work, both as a human responsibility and to attract people into the Communist Party, which embodied now, and would embody in the future, all the best qualities of humankind. [...]

We took it for granted that when the working class – or the blacks or any other disadvantaged people – took power, they would be inspired by only their purest and most distinguished ideals. [...]

The most powerful idea, the one that underpinned all the others, taken for granted and not even discussed, was that Capitalism was doomed, had been voted out by History itself. [13]

This is how Doris Lessing conceived the ideas of her communist milieu. She assumed that the British Communist Party alone could accomplish the desired objectives. We do not want to cast doubt on the idealism that inspired her to join the Party. Her enthusiasm was genuine. It would be impudent to ask, as Boswell did of Johnson, whether he would 'laugh at schemes of political improvement', and still more disrespectful to accept Johnson's response: 'Why, Sir, most schemes of political improvement are laughable things.' But Doris does seem to have judged things very one-sidedly. Was it simple intuition that drew her so strongly to the communists? She was certainly not given to self-questioning at the time. And yet, after four years of serving the Communist Party, it pained her to realize that, in Dr Johnson's words, a 'country governed by a despot is an inverted cone'.

Because of her communist sympathies, the British Secret Service kept an eye on Doris. They never restricted or interfered with her movements, but they diligently recorded them.

13   *Ibid.*, 280–6.

The Communist Party of Great Britain

The British Communist Party was founded in 1920 as part of the Soviet strategy for spreading revolution in Britain. The Party leadership was Moscow's tool. It received vast sums from the Communist International – £24,000 in 1921 alone (£500,000 in present-day values). Harry Pollitt, one of the secretaries trained at Moscow's International Lenin School, visited Moscow fifty times in the years after the Revolution. Another leader, J. T. Murphy, was on 'the directorate of the Lenin School, which trained cadres to defend a very Stalinized version of Bolshevism'.[1]

The British communists 'turned a blind eye towards' the Moscow trials at which prominent Soviet leaders were condemned to death for espionage. Behind this 'grisly facade of judicial murder, millions of Soviet citizens were imprisoned, killed or committed to internal exile'. Thus the British communists 'taught themselves to accept the lies that they heard from Moscow'.[2] When in 1956 Krushchev attacked Stalin's cult of personality and revealed the mass crimes Stalin had committed, Palme Dutt, a prominent Party member, wrote that those criticizing Stalin were 'ivory tower dwellers in fairyland'.[3] And when popular revolt broke out in East Berlin after Stalin's death, the British communists echoed the Moscow propaganda that the revolt was 'an attempted coup and fascist putsch'.[4] Many intellectuals who had been members of the Party submitted their resignations after the Soviet invasion of Hungary in 1956, but even after this event, the Party loyalists branded such critics of Soviet policy as middle-class defectors. It is true that, before this, many writers, historians, philosophers, and even scientists had joined the Party, 'inspired by altruistic, idealistic motives'. This idealism was thoroughly exploited by the Soviet

---

1 For details see: James Eaden and David Renton, *The Communist Party of Great Britain since 1920* (Basingstoke: Palgrave Macmillan, 2002), 21.
2 *Ibid.*, 65.
3 *Ibid.*, 119.
4 *Ibid.*, 118.

Secret Service to advance the cause of the Soviet Union. In 1990 it was publicly revealed how much 'Moscow's gold' had funded the activities of the British communists and how closely rank-and-file members had been working with the KGB. The British Communist party was dissolved in 1991 following the break-up of the Soviet Union.

MI5 – The British Security Service

The British security service, MI5 (Military Intelligence) was formally established in 1909 as an espionage bureau to counter the German intelligence operations developed by Kaiser Wilhelm II.[1] The tensions that led to World War I were already developing, and Wilhelm saw to the organization of a wide circle of spies in Great Britain to gather strategic information lest Germany should invade Britain. Such information had proved extremely effective in the rapid, crushing defeat the Germans had imposed on the French in the Franco-Prussian War of 1870–1. The Kaiser wanted to obtain all possible strategic military information for a future war that would possibly break out. MI5 was formed as a countermove to this scheme.

MI5 had had predecessors in two diminutive departments with other names. They were MO 2 and MO 3 ('MO' standing for 'Military Operations'). Both were founded at the War Office in 1903 to monitor the German naval build-up. MO 3 was renamed MO 5 in 1907 when it reported on operations during the Russo-Japanese War of 1904–5. MO 5 was eventually renamed MI5. With the outbreak of World War I, MI5 and its sister organization, the Secret Intelligence Service (SIS), extended their operations, becoming became 'more than national': they covered the British Empire and then Commonwealth, SIS becoming MI6.[2]

Recruiting

MI5 recruited its staff chiefly from army and navy officers who had gained some distinction in their careers, but Oxbridge graduates who had read Greats had easy access to the service as well. It was assumed that if they

1 Our source is the superb history of MI5 by Christopher Andrew, *The Defence of the Realm: The Authorized History of MI5* (Harmondsworth: Penguin Books, 2010).
2 *Ibid.*, xix.

were conversant in Greek and Latin literature and philosophy, they possessed rational and disciplined minds. One senior officer had read History
and had won the Gladstone Memorial Exhibition and an athletics blue at
Oxford. Other recruits were those who had been educated at Eton and at
Sandhurst Royal Military Academy, their 'recreations: riding, hunting,
point-to-point racing'.[3] It was (and perhaps still is) a myth favoured by the
upper-class mentality that such backgrounds equipped people for tasks in
government service. Many formidable intelligence officers in Germany,
Russia, the USA and Japan had never read Greats or practised point-
to-point racing, but still managed. MI5 did, however, place 'a premium
on foreign-language skills'. Because of rapid wartime expansion after
1915, women recruits were welcomed if personally recommended by ex-
isting members of staff. Leading girls' public schools were approached, as
were St Hugh's and Somerville Colleges at Oxford.[4] Recommendations
were taken up when, like one from the headmistress of Princess Helen's
College, Ealing, a reference spoke of a young woman's 'strong character'
and 'very straight, well disciplined, industrious' habits.[5] A high propor-
tion of upper-class female recruits came to play an important role in the
security service.

The 'Red Menace'

A Special Branch was created to look after suffragists, spies, anarchists
and individuals thought to pose a risk. This branch concentrated chiefly
on the significant threat posed by Soviet subversion. Once the Bolsheviks
had taken over power in Russia, Lenin sought to spread the Revolution
to the rest of Europe. In March 1919, the Communist International
(Comintern) was founded, under his direction, to carry forward this dis-
semination. Grigori Zinoviev, president of the Comintern, arrogantly

3   *Ibid.*, 135.
4   *Ibid.*, 60.
5   *Ibid.*, 122.

declared that all Europe would be communist within a year, and the Soviet-dominated executive committee of the Comintern issued instructions for achieving this at the Second Comintern Congress in Moscow in the summer of 1920. Members of the Comintern were obliged to support the Soviet Union unconditionally and by any means possible, legal or illegal. Systematic propaganda and agitation was to be spread within the armed forces, and communist cells were to be set up in every military unit. This work 'by Communists will for the most part have to be conducted illegally', the sponsors acknowledged.[6] Naturally MI5 regarded the idea of military subversion 'with peculiar horror',[7] and the service kept a vigilant eye on any pro-Bolshevik movements. This attention became close and immediate after the formation of the British Communist Party in 1920. MI5 began to monitor all 'known Communist front organizations in Britain, such as the National Minority Movement in the trade unions, as well as organizations with Communist affiliations, including Collet's Book Shop in London'.[8]

MI5 went on to take proactive, precautionary measures to control Bolshevik agents. When World War I came to an end, it compiled a 'Defence Black List' and then, in 1925, the 'Precautionary Index', which listed over 25,000 names. The index was divided into twelve categories ranging from 'persons connected with foreign secret service' organizations to 'persons of foreign blood or connection in the British Government civil service'. Within each category names were also 'grouped by races': it was 'not the nationality by place of birth, or by law, but nationality by blood, by racial interests, and by sympathy and friendship that [was] taken as the deciding factor in all classifications of possible enemy agents and dangerous persons'.[9]

Under MI5's surveillance came the editors of the communist oriented *Daily Herald*, and especially the pro-Bolshevik foreign editor of the paper, William Norman Ewer.[10] The Special Branch 'intercepted letters from British Communists, the Comintern and the Red International of Labour

6   Cited in *Ibid.*, 142.
7   *Ibid.*, 142.
8   *Ibid.*, 142.
9   *Ibid.*, 143.
10 *Ibid.*, 145.

Unions (RILU), minutes of the Politburo of the Communist Party of Great Britain (CPGB) and other Party committees, and reports from informers within the Communist Party and the trade unions'.[11] Recording of telephone conversations was a significant part of the surveillance. In 1924 an intercepted message from the communist provisional secretary of the London Transport Workers Solidarity Committee noted that 'We must be prepared to sabotage'. In 1930 MI5 and the Special Branch reported that:

> It is an indisputable fact that the British Communist Party, under instructions from Moscow, is endeavouring by every means possible to make such preparations that, in the event of war being declared by this country or in the event of a general mobilisation for war against Russia, chosen members of the Party should carry out previously arranged plans of sabotage. Definite orders have been issued from Moscow to the Communist Party of Great Britain (CPGB) that, in the event of a declaration of war, workers must be able to frustrate the campaign by general disorganisation.[12]

In the 1930s the British Fascist movement headed by Oswald Mosley was under close surveillance, but it was not ranked as a major threat to the country. The more important threat to British interests was seen to come from ever-increasing Nazi espionage. This danger claimed priority within MI5 and counter-operations were much intensified with the outbreak of war. The extensive activity of the German 'Fifth Column' in Britain caused a certain panic in MI5. The Fifth Column 'hysteria is reaching dangerous proportions', Home Intelligence reported.[13] To counter German intelligence, an Oxford don, J. C. N. Masterman, was employed to form what became a very effective institution: the Double-Cross System.[14] The task it undertook was to turn German spies into double-agents feeding false information to the Nazi regime. This deception proved highly successful during the war.

The effort to win the war took up nearly all of MI5's attention. Germany, Italy and Japan replaced Soviet Russia as the main targets of British foreign

11   *Ibid.*, 147–8.
12   Quoted in *Ibid.*, 166.
13   *Ibid.*, 223.
14   For details see: J. C. Masterman, *The Double-Cross System in the War of 1939 to 1945* (London: Sphere Books, 1973).

intelligence, and the Soviet menace slipped into fourth place in the SIS *Order of Priorities*.[15] The consequences were fatal: Soviet intelligence penetrated deep into the British security service.

The Gang from Trinity College, Cambridge

In the mid 1930s the Soviet security service succeeded in recruiting five Cambridge graduates from Trinity College: Kim Philby, Guy Burgess, Donald Maclean, Anthony Blunt and John Cairncross. These men began to work for Moscow, and are said to have been the 'ablest group of British agents ever recruited by a foreign power'.[16] They were also the most treacherous and most criminal – at least one of them, Kim Philby, had much blood on his hands. It took the British security service more than twenty years to unmask this group, whose identities were only discovered when a couple of Soviet agents defected from Moscow. This failure only shows how inefficient the British security service was and what a serious lack of professionalism remained within it. By the time the 'Magnificent Five'[17] were uncovered thousands of secret documents had been delivered to the Soviets. Blunt alone provided some 1,771 documents between 1941 and 1945.[18]

---

15 *Ibid.*, 195.
16 *Ibid.*, 420.
17 See 'The Hunt for the Magnificent Five', *Ibid.*, 420–41.
18 *Ibid.*, p. 272. For further reading see: Andrew Sinclair, *The Red and the Blue: Intelligence, Treason and the Universities* (London: Weidenfeld and Nicolson, 1986).

Secret Service Files

While she remained in Southern Rhodesia, Doris Lessing was unsettled and confused in mind. Her thoughts turned constantly to the idea of finding a new home in England. She would go 'with never a glance behind me. I was waiting for my future, my real life to begin. Behind me a door had slammed shut. [...] I was not going home to my family, I was fleeing from it. The door had shut and that was that.'[1] Her extraordinary life in England is related in Volume Two of her remarkable autobiography.[2] In this book she also tells us about her interest in Communism, giving us an idea about how active she was within the British Communist Party. The Secret Service reports corroborate this, documenting her precise movements, whom she met, and what she said. They begin almost as soon as she arrived. The Rhodesian Security Liaison Office reported to the Director General of the security service in London, informing him that Mrs Lessing had sailed from Cape Town for the UK about the middle of March 1949 with the intention of taking employment in England. London soon confirmed that 'the Subject entered England on 28th April 1949'.

This is where our records begin. The Rhodesian Secret Service had kept an eye on Doris right from the day she had been noticed as a person working with the local communists. Even after she had left Salisbury the Secret Service maintained close contact with MI5. All these reports have now been released, and are accessible at the National Archives, Kew, Richmond, Surrey. The sources of information are: The Security Service Personal Files – Communists and Suspected Communists, Including Russian and Communist Sympathisers: *Doris May Lessing*. The references within this set are: KV2/4054; KV2/4055; KV2/4056; KV2/4057; and KV2/4058. The reports pertinent to our purpose are reproduced in the next section in chronological order.

1   Lessing, *Under My Skin*, 418–9.
2   Lessing, *Walking in the Shade. Volume Two of My Autobiography, 1949–1962* (London: Flamingo, 1998).

The Files on Doris Lessing (chronological)

Early Security Interest

1943

File No. SF 411/S. Rhodesia
Extract for File No. 97, 471
Lessing
Dated: 23.3.43

X. Ref. to letter which was intercepted by the
S.A. censorship from Lessing.
On 23.3.43 a letter was intercepted by the South
African Censorship from Doris M. Wisdom dated 18.1.43.
It was addressed to the *Guardian*, 6 Barrack Street,
Cape Town, and contained a report on Communist or-
ganisation in Southern Rhodesia. It was originally
written in English.

1944

I.

File No. SF 411/S. Rhodesia
Extract for File No. 97, 471
Dated: 26.9.44
Extract from a letter from Air Ministry, Adastral
House, Kingsway, W.C. 2 re Salisbury Left Club
mentioning the Lessings

This club in Salisbury, Southern Rhodesia, has
been brought to our attention by our DAPM with the

Rhodesian Air Training Group. The club is controlled
by a Mr & Mrs Lessing, the former being a German, and
the latter a South African. The club is patronised
by persons with foreign accents, and also a certain
number of casual and regular RAF personnel. The general tone of the club is reported to be very left,
and it is stated that most topics of discussion there
usually end up in anti-British, anti-capitalist and
anti-imperialist vapourings.

2.

File No. SF 411/S. Rhodesia
Extract for File No. 97, 471
Lessing
21st October 1944

Dear Major Clemow,
    We have corresponded in the past about the branch
of the Left Book Club which was started in Salisbury
in 1938.
    The Air Ministry now informs us that a number of
RAF men, chiefly members of the Rhodesian Air Training
Group, are frequenting the Club which is now under the
direction of Mr & Mrs Lessing; the former is a German
and the latter a South African. The Club is said to
be patronised by persons with foreign accents and its
general tone is very 'left'; in the course of most
of its discussions anti-British and anti-imperialist
views are expressed. In view of this we should be very
much interested to have some up to date information
about the club and its activities. We have record of
a certain Mrs Gwendoline Margaret Lessing alias Gwen
Haggis, who was born at Johannesburg on 2.9.17 and was
formerly a dancer at the Casino at Lorenzo Marques.
There seems just a possibility that this may be the
Mrs Lessing in question.

The Left Book Club in this country ceased to exist shortly after the outbreak of war, but until that time it was working so closely with the Communist Party as to be in effect a Communist subsidiary organisation. When the Communist Party adopted its anti-war policy however, the Left Book Club leader and publisher Victor Gollancz refused to conform and withdrew his cc-operation, with the result the whole organisation collapsed. There is therefore no parent body in England with which the Salisbury Club can now communicate.

Yours sincerely

Brigadier Sir David Petrie

Major H. W. Clemow, OBE
Chief Superintendent CID
BSA Police
Box 583
Bulawayo

3.

SF 411/S. Rhodesia
Extract for File No. 97, 471
Dated: 24ᵗʰ October 1944

Dear Bulkley,

Many thanks for your PM1/IS/13/10 of 26.9.44 relating to the Salisbury Left Club and for giving me details regarding the airmen accustomed to patronise this establishment.

It appears we have no traces of any of the airmen concerned and I do not think that any action from an Internal Security point of view is necessary at the present time though I shall naturally be glad to hear if any of the airmen come to notice in a communist connection in the future which RAF censorship may quite possibly disclose. I am having some enquiries made regarding Mr & Mrs Lessing, the controllers of the club, as it seems possible that these people have come to our notice in the past. This fact, however, will be established as the result of their enquiries and any information thus obtained I will naturally pass on to you.

Yours sincerely,

Edward A. H. Oddy

Squadron Leader A. F. Bulkley
AIR MINISTRY

4.

SF 411/S. Rhodesia
Extract for File No. 97, 471
Dated: 27.11.44
Extract from a report from Civil Security Bureau, Southern Rhodesia re The Salisbury Club, mentioning the Lessings.

The leading light in the Salisbury Left Club is Doris May Lessing, nee Taylor, formerly Wisdom, a British subject by birth, born at Kermanshah, Persia, on 22.10.1919. Mrs Lessing who is employed as a typist with a firm of Solicitors, married Gottfried Anton Nicolai Lessing, a German refugee of Jewish extraction, born Leningrad, 14.12.1914, at Salisbury on 15.1.1944. Lessing, a solicitor's clerk, has been resident of Southern Rhodesia since 10.3.1939 and his wife since 1924. Mrs Lessing, who also takes an active part in the affairs of the Salisbury Branch of the Rhodesian Friends of the Soviet Union, is a member of the propaganda committee of the Rhodesian Labour Party.

1947

SF 411/S. Rhodesia
Extract for File No. 97, 471
Dated: 6.10.47
Extract from a report on Communism in Southern Rhodesia, forwarded by British South African Police Headquarters, dated 6.10.47, mentioning the Lessings.

COMMUNISM IN SOUTHERN RHODESIA
RE: PERSONS OF SUSPECTED COMMUNIST TENDENCIES

Lessing, Doris May: Formerly Wisdom, born Iran. Wife of Gottfried Anton Nicolai Lessing, a German born in Russia. Active Leftist and Trade Unionist. Correspondent of Betty Radford of the Cape Town *Guardian* – distributed copies of *Guardian* in Salisbury early part of war. Connected with RFSU [Rhodesian Friends of the Soviet Union]. Husband is reported to have communist leanings.

P.O. Box 452 Salisbury

1949

Security Liaison Office
P.O. Box 683
Salisbury
Southern Rhodesia
PF 86
Dated: 21st April 1949

The Director-General of the Security Service,
(Attention of G. T. D. Patterson, Esq.)
Box 357, GPO
London, E.C. 1.

1. Mrs Doris May Lessing (formerly Wisdom, nee Taylor) born at Karmanshah, Persia, on 22.10.19, holder of the Southern Rhodesian Passport No. 45037 issued at Salisbury on 13.12.48 is reported to have sailed from Cape Town for the U.K. about the middle of March with the intention of taking employment in England. Mrs Lessing has been married and divorced twice. Her first husband was Frank Charles Wisdom; her second, Gottfried Anton Nicolai Lessing, a German refugee whom she married in 1944. The second divorce took place last year.

2. Mrs Lessing is reported to have been a member of the Rhodesian Friends of the Soviet Union during the war, to have been a correspondent of the South African Communist Betty Radford, and to have distributed *The Guardian* in Salisbury. Both she and her most recent husband are members of a group of suspected Communist sympathisers responsible for a new periodical called Nota Bene.

3. I think it is likely that Mrs Lessing will get in touch with the British Communist Party, possibly even with Party Headquarters, and I should be grateful if you would keep a look-out for her.

Security Liaison Officer,
Central Africa
(C. A. G. Simkins)

Heightened Interest and the Authors' World Peace Delegation

1950

I.

Commander,
Special Branch
Dated: 27.3.50

Doris May Lessing

20 Benbigh Road,
London, W.1

Gottfried Anton Nicolai
Lessing
30 Steeles Road,
London, N.W.3.

Doris May Lessing, nee Taylor, formerly Wisdom, was a British subject by birth and was born in Persia on 22 October 1919. She was divorced by her second husband Gottfried Anton Nicolai Lessing during 1948. Mrs Lessing arrived in this country from South Africa in April 1949.

Gottfried Anton Nicolai Lessing was German by birth and was born at Leningrad, Russia on 14 December 1914; he arrived in the country from South Africa in May 1949. It is possible that he is now a British Subject.

According to information we have received, both Mr and Mrs Lessing are known for their Communist activities in Southern Rhodesia and we would be glad to know if they should come to your notice whilst in this country.

G. R. Lee

2.

To: SLO Central Africa
From: Director General
Dated: 22.6.50
Please refer to your PF 86 of 21 April 1949.

Source CHEST reports that Moses M. Kotane, General Secretary of the late Communist Party of South Africa, has informed Maud Rogerson, of Communist Party Headquarters in London, that Comrade Godfrey [sic] Lessing is known personally to him and has directed all his activities 'in the interests of the Labour Movement'. Another reliable source reports that Lessing was registered as a member of the British Communist Party for 1950.

   Doris May Lessing has not come to notice since her arrival in this country.

   We have not passed on this information to the South African Police and invite you to do so at your own discretion.

   Director General

3.

Metropolitan Police
Special Branch
Dated: 27 June 1950
To: BIA
Ref. PF 97, 471

With reference to MI5 letter No. PF 9741/B.1.a./GRL, dated 27th March 1950, asking whether Gottfried Anton Nicolai Lessing of 30, Steeles Road, N.W.3, and Doris May Lessing of 20, Denbigh Road, W.1, have come to notice in this country in connection with Communist activities:

Gottfried Anton Nicolai Lessing was born in Leningrad on 14th December 1914, and was of German nationality. He became a naturalised British subject by virtue of a certificate of naturalisation issued in Southern Rhodesia on 6th November 1948. He arrived in the United Kingdom in May 1949, travelling on Southern Rhodesian passport No. 44575, issued on 11th November 1948.

Lessing continues to reside at 30, Steeles Road, where he occupies a furnished bed-sitting room. He describes himself as a solicitors' clerk, but as far as can be asserted, he has not been employed in any capacity since his arrival in this country. He is recently reported to have spent some time in hospital, and to have made at least two visits to the continent, to Belgium and Holland.

Extensive enquiries have been made, but no evidence is forthcoming to show that he is actively connected with the Communist Party, and he has not hitherto come to the notice of Special Branch. However, during the course of enquiries, it was ascertained that a G. A. Lessing, who may well be identical with the subject of the enquiry, was responsible for auditing the yearly accounts of the St Pancras Branch of the Communist Party.

Further, it is of interest to note that Lessing is reported to be on friendly terms with Helgar and John Derry Chinnery, who also reside at the same address. The former took part in the lobbying of M.P.s in connection with the Peace Campaign on 14th March 1950, and was similarly active on behalf of the Student Labour Federation. This latter is reported to be a member of the British China Conference Committee, and a member of the Communist Committee to promote relations with the new China (400/49/508 refers).

Doris May Lessing, formerly Wisdom, nee Taylor arrived in the United Kingdom in April 1949, and resided at 20, Denbigh Road, W.1 until June 1949, when she removed to her present address, 5, Westbourne Terrace, W. 2. Despite extensive enquiries, nothing has been learned about her activities in any connection. As far as can be ascertained, she has no regular employment, and is frequently away from her address. She has not previously come under notice of Special Branch.

Gottfried Lessing and his ex-wife Doris May Lessing arrived in this country separately, and, during the course of enquiries, nothing has come to light to indicate that they have since been in regular contact with each other.

Only Gottfried Lessing is known to me, and his description is:
Aged 35, 5′ 8-9″, slim build, hair fair, thin and receding in front, eyes blue, wears glasses, tanned complexion, speaks English with a very slight trace of foreign accent.
P. S.
Submitted.
Chief Inspector.
Chief Superintendent.

1951

I.

File No. PF 72, 297
Dated: 6.3.51
Extract from SLO Southern Rhodesia re Zelter Communist sympathiser, mentioning Nicolai Lessing and Doris May Lessing.

This man and his wife are reputed to be pro-Soviet in outlook and they have a number of Communist friends, including Gottfried Anton Nicolai Lessing and Doris May Lessing nee Wisdom, both of whom have PE's [Personal File entries] in Head Office.

2.

File No. PF 73, 415
Dated: 1.4.51
1/c call for ILSE from unidentified man with a foreign accent.

Distant is told that Ilse left for Germany three days ago. *Distant* wants to know if 'Uraine' went with her. The reply is in the affirmative. *Distant* asks for Ilses's address. It is 'c/o K. [or possibly T.] Lessing, Berlin, Nikolasee, Barnische Alle [Benschallee] 162, S. Sector.'

3.

File No. PF 73, 415
Receipt Date: 3.4.51
Cross reference to telegram despatched to H.Q. Intelligence Div:

70 E.Q. CCG/BE BAOR, 15, saying that Dadoo left for Prague on 29th March 1951, Address in Eastern Zone given as c/o K. Lessing, Berlin, Nikolasee, Barnische Allee [Benschallee] 162.

4.

File No. PF 73, 415
Lessing
Dated: 4th April 1951

Dear Colonel Allan,

In confirmation of my telephone message, I would
be grateful if you would now transfer the HOW [Home
Office Warant] on Ilse Dadoo (Reference 11 065) to c/o
Lessing, Berlin, Nikolassee, Barnische (or Bahnische)
Allee [Benschallee], 162, Soviet sector.

I am applying for an extension of the HOW to
cover 'Any name' at this address as I am interested
in Lessing, whom I believe to be a South African
Communist, possibly collaborating with Dadoo.

Yours sincerely,

Signed. C. P. C de Wesselow

Colonel M. F. Allan, MBE

GPO

5.

File No. PF 73, 415
Lessing
Dated: 4th April 1951

Further to my letter of this reference dated 20th
March 1951, Ilse Dadoo left for Prague on 29th March
accompanied by her seven year daughter Shiren and she
said that she was on her way to the Eastern Zone of
Berlin and that she would be away for six to eight
months before returning to the U.K.

We have now learnt that her address in Berlin will
be c/o Lessing, Berlin, Nikolassee, Barnische Allee
[Benschallee], 162.

In view of the international ramifications of the
case, we are suggesting to Int. Div. that it would be
better handled by yourselves than by them.

Yours sincerely,

Signed. C. P. C. de Wesselow

6.

Extract from File No. PF 97, 471
Name: Lessing
Dated: 6.4.51
Secret
To the Postmaster-General, and all others who may be
concerned:

I hereby authorize and require you to detain, open
and produce for my inspection all postal packets and
telegrams addressed to:
   'Any Name'
   Berlin, Nicolassee
   Bernische Allee [Benschallee] 162
or to any name at that or any other address if there
is a reasonable ground to believe that they are intended for the said address and for so doing this
shall be your sufficient Warrant.
   This is the new address of a leading South African
communist (subject of HOW number 11065) who has been
organising communist activities among South Africans
in the United Kingdom in connection with the British
Communist Party. It is desired to continue to investigate her activities and contacts since her letters
may not be addressed to her by name it is required to
extend the warrant.
   One of
   His Majesty's Principal Secretaries of State

7.

File No. PF 217, 290 (Smith, L. E. W.)
Lessing
Dated: 9.8.51
Extract from S.B.Report forward by C. C. Somerset re
SMITH, ment. [mentioning] Lessing.

He is on extremely friendly terms with Dorothy Lessing, an authoress, of 71, Church Street, London, W.8., who is responsible for the book 'The Grass is Singing'. Mrs Lessing has visited him on several occasions, and they correspond frequently.

In letters he has received from Dorothy Lessing, whom he calls 'Trigger', there does not seem to be anything strongly suggestive that she is interested in Communism.

8.

File No. 771, 030.
Lessing, G.A.N.
Dated: 30.8.51
Extract from S.B. Report re Gottfried Anton Nicolai Lessing (Communist) mentioning his wife, Doris Lessing

Neither Lessing nor his former wife Dorothy May Lessing has come to the notice of Special Branch since the last report dated 29.6.50 on file No. 402/50/398. Mrs Lessing is now living at 71, Church St., W. 8.

9.

To: SLO Central Africa
29th November 1951
From: Director General

According to Seat, a friend of Dorothy Schwartz, whose name source gives only as 'Tia', has been helping Schwartz, and through her the Communist Party, to contact Charles Mzingeli during his visit here.

Apart from the fact that she is a former member of the Southern Rhodesian Labour Party, we have no further particulars of her and cannot identify her on this information. Have you any suggestions, please?

10.

Security Liaison Office
P.O. Box 683
Salisbury, Southern Rhodesia
Dated: 18ᵗʰ December 1951
Ref. PF 84, 430
The Director General of the Security Service,
London

Please refer to your PF 84,430/B.1.g/CPCdeW of 29ᵗʰ November 1951.The BSA Police report as follows:

I have no record of 'Tea'[1] but am of the impression that the contact with Dorothy Schwartz is more than likely Mrs Doris May Lessing, who was known by the names 'Tig', 'Tigs' and 'Tigger'. It is likely that your source may have been confused between 'Tia' and 'Tig'.

It will be recalled that Charles Mzingeli stated in his letter to the 'African Weekly' (see my PF 77 of [date unclear] December 1951) that he was being taken by Dorothy Schwartz to Mrs Lessing's premises for dinner.

Mrs Lessing was a former member of the Southern Rhodesian Labour Party and in 1944 was a member of the 'Labour Party Propaganda Committee'.

Security Liaison Officer,
Central Africa,
(B. M. de Quehen)

---

1   'Further to my PF 201 of 18th December 1951, Mrs Doris May Lessing was known locally as *Tia*': B. M. Quehen, Security Liaison Office, Salisbury, PF 86, 28.12.1951 to The Director-General of the Security Service, London.

II.

Security Liaison Office
P.O. Box 683
Salisbury, Southern Rhodesia
Dated: 28th December 1951
Ref. PF 84, 430

The Director-General of the Security Service,
London

Further to my PF 201 of 18th December 1951, Mrs Doris
May Lessing was known locally as 'Tia'.
    Security Liaison Officer,
    Central Africa,
    (B. M. de Quehen)

1952

I.

Security Liaison Office
P.O. Box 683
Salisbury, Southern Rhodesia
19th February 1952
PF 86

The Director-General of the Security Service,
London
Your reference PF 97,471/BIA/JHM of 22.6.50.

Local Swift reports that Mrs Doris May Lessing, the
novelist and author of 'Rustling Grass' [sic], is very
friendly with Phyllis Monica Loveridge of Salisbury
and with Carol Nathan and Dorothy Zelter. She has let
them know that she intends to visit East Germany with

an unknown male friend for three weeks in the near future. There she intends meeting some 'big bugs' which may result in a play of hers being produced in the Eastern Zone. She hopes to meet 'Gottfried' (her husband) from whom she has not heard for a long time, chiefly she thinks, because he is doing something in the interior, and feels it safer not to write from East to West. Doris thinks that communications with the West are, understandably, suspect.

Charles Mzingeli saw Mrs Lessing three times in London – her address is 71, Church Street, W. 8, and told her that the Moral Rearmament people shook him with their anti-Soviet propaganda.

B. M. de Quehen,
Security Liaison Officer,
Central Africa

2.

PF 97, 471/B.1.g/CPCdeW
Dated: 11ᵗʰ March 1952

With further reference to correspondence about Gottfried Anthony Lessing (your last reference [*sic*])

We have now learnt that his ex-wife Doris May Lessing, mentioned in our letter PF 97,471/B.1.b/JK dated 7ᵗʰ July 1951 as a suspected communist, proposes to visit Berlin for three weeks in the near future with an unidentified male friend. According to a reliable and delicate source she hopes to meet Gottfried, from whom she has not heard for a long time, mainly, she believes, because he is doing something in the interior and feels it safer not to write to the West.

Doris Lessing is the author of various novels and hopes to make high-level contacts which will result in the production in the Eastern Zone of a play she has written. She is on fairly close terms with Dorothy Schwartz and has on occasion given her assistance in communist activities, and it is fairly certain from her record that, if not a Party member, she is very close to the Party.

We still have no news of the exact whereabouts of Gottfried Lessing. It may be of interest, however, that in May last he was in touch with a person whose name and address were given as Zurchov, Berlin W.8, Tarlenstrasse [perhaps Tannenstrasse] 10. I should be interested to hear whether Zurchov is known to you, if you can identify him.

Yours sincerely,

C. P. C. de Wesselow

3.

Temple Bar 2151 (Communist Party H.Q.)
Incoming. 14.5 52
Doris Lessing rang Sam Aaronovitch and said that Joan Rodker wanted her to see him. She arranged to come on Monday morning at 10.30, the 19th.

Sam asked if she had a card [communist Membership card] and she said she had not yet but expected it would turn up in due course. [Indistinct].

4.

File No. PF 704, 051 Name: Lacey, Doris
Responsible Section BIF/MBT
Date of letter: 20.5.52

15.35 Both conversations were going full blast at this point and it became impossible to make out what Cox and Schwartz were discussing. Later on, she said: 'There is another matter I want to raise – that is application (?)[2] of Doris Lacey (?)'. It was gathered

2   The question marks (?) indicating uncertainty appear in the original files.

that this woman wanted to join the Party and that she had written a book. Schwartz did not think much of the latter but said that Maud (Rogerson) had been rather impressed with it (think) [*sic*]. Cox suggested that, as Lacey's (?) interests were literary, perhaps she had better see Sam Aaronovitch. Apparently, she was already in touch with him, which seemed to surprise Cox.

15.40 (Parrish's conversation again became predominant.) Schwartz evidently continued to speak of Lacey (?), however. She gave her address: [illegible] Terrace (rest of street name drowned), Kensington, W. 8. She also volunteered the information that Lacey (?) had a child.

5.

NOTE
Dated: 27 June 1952

Mr Roach telephoned this morning to say that he had read in the *Daily Telegraph* that six writers were forming a delegation to the World Meeting of Authors which is to be held tomorrow in Moscow. Three of the six, Arnold Kettle, Naomi Mitchison and A. E. Coppard, are known to IRD, but the other three, Richard Mason, Doris Lessing and Douglas Young, are not.

I gave IRD the following information over the telephone:

Richard Mason is N.T:

Doris Lessing is the author of several novels and is believed to be a close sympathiser, who recently planned to have her plays produced in the Eastern Zone of Germany.

Douglas Young, a one time Chairman of the Scottish National Party for whom he stood unsuccessfully at Kirkalady [*sic*] in 1945. He was described in 1945 by the *Observer* as a classical gallic scholar with some erudition and a pamphleteer and traveller.

6.

File No. 52988
SB report Northholt Airport
Dated: 28.6.52
*Extract from SB Northolt Airport Report re Members of
the Authors' World Peace Appeal leaving for Brussels
en route for Moscow, mentioning Lessing.*

The under mentioned members of the Authors World
Peace Appeal left Airport for Brussels at 9.30 a.m.
to-day en route for Moscow.
   [...]
   Lessing, Miss Doris May (402/50/398) born 22.10.19
   British Passport No. 1553
   According to present arrangements this delegation
was returning to the U.K. on 16.7.52.

7.

PF 97, 471
Lessing
Dated: 27.6.52
*Extract from letter to Room 055 Office from [name
erased] offering to give information to the Security
Service, mentioning Doris Lessing and her husband.*

68, Barons Court Rd., Kensington, W.14.

Doris Lessing (whose second husband, a Communist, now
lives in Eastern Sector of Germany) flies tomorrow
morning (Saturday) to Prague and then to Moscow, part
of a Russian Authors' sponsored Delegation visiting
Russia.
   Yours faithfully
   [name erased]

8.

PF 97, 471
Lessing
17.7.52
Extract from S.B. [Special Branch] report re Meeting of Authors' World Peace Appeal held on 17 July 1952, mentioning Lessing.

A meeting of the Authors' World Peace Appeal (400/ 51/194) held in the 'Small Meeting House' at Friends House, Euston Road at 7.30 p.m. on Thursday, 17th July 1952 to 10 p.m.

The purpose of the meeting was to enable an account to be given of experiences of a party of British writers who had been invited by Nikolai Tikhonov on behalf of the Union of Soviet Writers to meet their opposite numbers in Moscow. [...]

The Chairman was Alex Comfort (RF 405/42/238) and on the platform with him were the following members of the party who had just returned from Moscow and Prague: [...], Lessing, Doris May (PF 402/50/398), [...].

Both Lessing and Mason spoke about their impressions and that the Russian people talked Peace and not war, all the efforts of the people were diverted to peaceful tasks and not one member of the Party had any indication of war preparation – the idea had been shown to be too fantastic for serious consideration. [...].

9.

PF 704, 051
Lacey
Dated: 30.7.52

I should be most grateful if you could possibly find out if a woman whose name I believe to be Doris Lacey,

an authoress, was staying at Alexa Hotel, Lexham
Gardens on about 12th May last. She is probably a
Rhodesian or South African. She has a child.
    C. P. C. de Wesselow

10.

11th August 1952
Re: Doris Lacey
? staying at Alexa Hotel,
71, Lexham Gardens, W. 8.

I have inspected the register at the Alexa Hotel for
the months of March, April, May and June 1952 but
could find no record of the above-named person having
stayed there during that period.
    B.I.G. (Mr C. P. C. de Wesselow)

Your memo., PF704,051 dated 30.7.1952 refers.
D. Storrier

11.

PF 97, 471
Miss Doris Lessing
Dated: 29.9.52
*Extract from MI6 Report re: United Kingdom. Counter
Espionage Character Sketches of Members of the British
Authors' Deputation to Moscow. Mentioning: Miss Doris
Lessing.*

1. We give below a short description of the political affiliations of the six British authors who recently paid a visit to Moscow between 29 June and 13th
July 1952.
    [...]

(c) Miss Doris Lessing. A novelist. Certainly pro communist, but doubtful if she is a member of the Party. Her communist sympathies have been fanned almost to the point of fanaticism owing to her upbringing in Rhodesia, which has brought out in her a deep hatred of the colour bar. Colonial exploitation is her pet theme and she has now nearly become as irresponsible in her statements as Coppard saying that everything black is wonderful and that all men and all things white are vicious.

12.

Security Liaison Office,
P.O. Box 683
Salisbury, Southern Rhodesia
Dated: 21st August 1952

The Director-General of the Security Service,
London

Doris May Lessing
Further to my PF 86 of 19.2.52 and your PF 97,471. It has been reported in the Rhodesian *Sunday Mail* on 28.7.52 that Mrs Lessing visited Russia and Czechoslovakia on a 17-day tour with five other British writers, Mrs Naomi Mitchison, A. E. Coppard, Douglas Young, Arnold Kettle and Richard Mason. They went at the invitation of the Union of Soviet Writers and as delegates of the authors' World Peace Appeal.

It was further reported in the *New Statesman and Nation* dated the 12th July 1952, under the advertisements dealing with meetings and lectures that 'A. E. Coppard, Doris Lessing and Arnold Kettle' would hold a meeting at the SCR 14, Kensington Square, W. 8 on the 20th July (Sunday), 1952, to discuss with Soviet Writers their recent tour to the Soviet Union.

However, I expect you are already well aware of
this activity. In view of Mrs Lessing's continued association with Southern Rhodesia (where she was born)
I should be grateful if you could send me a report on
her more recent doings, if you have such a thing, for
the information of the BSA Police.
Security Liaison Officer,
Central Africa
(B. M. de Quehen)

13.

PF 97, 471/B.1.g/PBR.
To: SLO Central Africa
From: Director General
Dated: 11th September 1952

Doris May Lessing
Please refer to your PF. 86 dated 21st August 1952 in
which you ask for a report on subject's more recent
doings. We have the following will suit your purpose.
   Subject entered England on 28th April 1949. Her
occupation is given as typist. She did not come to
notice until April 1951 when a review on a book by
her appeared in the *Daily Worker*. In November 1951
she again came to notice under the name 'Tia' as as-
sisting Dorothy Schwartz, and through her the British
Communist Party, to contact Charles Mzingeli during a
visit to England. In February 1952 it was learnt that
she proposed to visit Berlin and hoped there to meet
her former husband, Gottfried Anton Nicolai Lessing,
a known member of the British Communist Party. She
hoped also that her visit would enable her to make
contacts which would result in the production in the
Eastern Zone of a play which she had written. In June
she went to Moscow as one of a number of members of
the Authors' World Peace Appeal who attended a World
meeting of Authors. In July she spoke in London at a

small meeting of the Authors' World Peace Appeal and gave her impression of her visit to Russia.

Doris Lessing has been described as certainly pro-communist although it is doubtful if she is a party member. Her Rhodesian background has brought out in her deep hatred of the colour bar which has reached the point of fanaticism. In this way her communist sympathies have been increased.

for Director General
[signature illegible]

14.

Security Liaison Office
P.O. Box 683
Salisbury,
Southern Rhodesian
Dated: 24th September 1952
The Director General of the Security Service,
London

Mrs. Doris May Lessing
Thank you very much for your PF 97471/B1G/PBR of 11 September 1952, which I have passed over to my police links. They have told me that Doris Lessing has sent Charles Mzingeli an account of her recent travels in Russia, France and Italy. The main theme is the superiority of living conditions and educational development in the Soviet Union compared with other European countries and Africa.

She has also become a member of the Fabian Colonial Bureau and corresponds with Elias Mtepuka of the Nyasaland African Congress, and Lawrence Vambe of the 'African Weekly'. She is also in touch with the Zelters (now back in Southern Rhodesia) and Dorothy Schwartz. Mrs Lessing is sending political publications, probably translations of Russian works, to Mtepuka to be passed on to Charles Mzingeli.

Security Liaison Officer,
Central Africa
(B. M. de Quehen)

15.

Temple Bar 2151
(Communist Party Headquarters)
Incoming 4.10.52

Doris Lessing for Sam Aaronovitch to know whether
he would be free on November 24th for a meeting at
8.30 p.m.
    Sam said that he was.
    Doris would send out notices. She told Sam that she
was anxious to get in touch with Desmond or someone as
she was receiving letters asking for advice and she
wanted to discuss them with someone. Sam said that he
would put her on to Idris.
    Doris spoke to Idris and told him that she would
like to come and discuss something with him fairly
soon. She was getting letters asking for advice and
she wanted to consult with him what she ought to say.
    Idris arranged to see her on Thursday at twelve
o'clock.

16.

PF 97, 471
Lessing
Jarvis
Ibbetson
Milne

Vienna British Preparations
Serial: 37c
Receipt Date: 19.11.52

Extract from B1F Source report re Vienna Peace
Congress.

Vienna Peace Congress
1. The following are additional sponsors for the
Congress whose names it is believed have not been
published:
    Doris Lessing

Comments by Section of Origin
Source reliable

17.

19.11.52

o/g call to Templebar 2151 from Hymie Fagan asking for
James Klugman who is not there. Hymie gets through
to Sam. Sam thinks James will be in this morning.
Sam asks Hymie how his school got on, Hymie says it
was postponed till the 29th and 30th — Eric postponed
it. Hymie tells Sam he has still got his copy of the
Economist. 09.58
    o/g call to Western 1571 from Hymie Fagan asking
for Eleanor Fox who is not in. Hymie says to some woman
that he wanted to know the address of Doris Lessing.
He is told that she apparently lives with Joan Rooker
so they must get a card out for her (Doris). Hymie
says he does not know Joan Rooker's address, they go
to look it up for him: 71, Church Street W. 8.

18.

Note for PF 97, 471
29.11.52

Hymie Fagan (P F39, 815), a longstanding member of the
British Communist Party, is the subject of a current

telephone check in order to clarify his present activities. It seems that he is undertaking checking
up enquiries on certain persons, but on whose instructions he is doing this is not at present clear.
In this work he has been collaborating with James
Klugmann (Education Department of the C. P.) and
Betty Reid, who is responsible for the security of
Party personnel. He maintained contact with Korovin,
Councillor at the Soviet Embassy, who has recently
returned to the USSR. and is in touch with Bruslov,
First Secretary in charge of cultural affairs. He was
until the beginning of this year Assistant Secretary
of the British Soviet Friendship Society and still
carries out many activities on behalf of this organisation. His wife, Maggie Evans, PF 296, 505, has
South African family connections. Dorothy Schwartz,
who I see is known to Doris Lessing, was staying with
the Fagans in October this year.

D. Mumford

19.

Extracted for File No. PF 97, 471
Name: Doris Lessing
Dated: 6.11.52
Responsible Section: B.1.A/AJ
Date of Delivery: 24.11.52

12.10. Cox talking with Dorothy (?Woodman)? (Doris
Lessing) almost certainly D. Lessing. The conversation was already in progress.

She was speaking about Charles Mzingeli, who had
been over here last year, whom she had seen and who
was a personal friend of hers. She had brought with
her a letter which she had either written to Mzingeli
or to an African friend of hers which she asked Cox
to read.

There was a break in the conversation.

When picked up again she was evidently speaking of Mzingeli again. She said that 'he' knew that she was COMMUNIST. They had worked together for some time. She said that he was really a 'very moral person'. When he had been over here he had been in great confusion of mind as regarded the Soviet Union. He was 'very religious' and had been in touch with the OXFORD GROUP and appeared to have been impressed by them.

She had also met with an African of the name of Indekukko (?). (This is not distinct and phonetic as far as possible). He had been on a delegation to COPAI.

At this point Cox interrupted her to ask a question about a man and his wife of whom she had evidently been speaking to him previously. Doris (?) said that this man was now a 'rich business man' but he was O.K. and politically sound. His wife was O.K. too.

Cox said that he thought this man had been along to a conference organised by the UDC. There were all sorts of people and Movements, Cox said, in Africa who were progressive but not yet prepared to associate openly with the Communist Party. In the case of such people, he said, we have adopted the practice of letting them write to our people in an individual capacity and our people write back to them! In the absence of any broad movement in Britain on African problems, they could not be expected to contact the Communist Party as such. The Party had to regard with reserve the activities Fenner Brockway and the Congress of Peoples Against Imperialism. They had no actual proof that the Americans were behind this, but they noticed that Brockway always refrained from criticising the Americans. In North Africa, where the Movement had the strongest support, quite obviously, the Americans, in their own interests, were giving some kind of secret backing to the so-called National Movement. Therefore there was always a danger in these people going to the Congress of Peoples Against Imperialism and contacting Brockway. (Cox made some indistinct references to Basil Davidson but this could not be followed.)

Cox went on to tell the visitor that it would be very helpful to the [word missing], if when she had letters, she would consult the Centre.

After this the conversation became indistinct again. Cox could be heard referring to the case of Zukas and of someone approaching Arthur Horner and Attlee on his behalf.

The visitor then returned to the subject of the African, Indekkko (Katilungu – PF). She said that he had a very good brain and was very clear. After meeting the visitor he had written to her. It seemed he wanted to come back to England. One of his letters had annoyed her very much. It seemed that he was inclined to be a bit anti-White. She had written him a very strong letter. He was anxious to train for leadership. The visitor seemed to think that he was worth training. They discussed the possibility of a scholarship for him. She thought he should not be wasted. Cox said that of course there had been an arrangement for training Colonial people in Prague and in Eastern Berlin which had been initiated some three or four years before. There were actually five Nigerians now, three in Prague and two in Berlin. But the scheme had now been virtually dropped. It had led to many complications. But that was a long story. There had been the impression in West Africa as to how scholarships could be obtained. In any case it was now obvious that as far as Prague and Eastern Germany were concerned, they were no longer anxious to have Africans. The trouble was that comrades who had gone there tended to become isolated from their own people and also they became 'glamourized' and got swelled heads. He understood that WFTU had now considered a scheme for the granting of three months course of study, but they were writing for some more precise information. This might be the best course for Indekokku (?) – (Katilungu).

The conversation now became indistinct and difficult to follow. Cox said that he did not think anything could be done for Indekuko (?) (Katilungu) by the C. P. as such. The proper channel would be WFTU, or through the National Union of Mineworkers in this country. (This referred to Zukas.) The visitor asked what had happened to him now, and Cox said that an order had been given for his deportation. Cox thought he was out of prison now.

Reverting to Indekukko (?) (Katilungu), Cox told the visitor that she should write to him and find out if he could be sponsored by some organisation, perhaps a Trade Union or the National Movement in order to see if he could get some kind of scholarship.

12.27. The visitor left.

12.59. Cox could be heard telling Dutt that Doris Lessing (?), Dorothy Woodman (?) had been in there that morning. He explained [...] her friendship with Mzingeli of Southern Rhodesia and of her wish to help another African, a friend of Mzingeli's who wanted to come over to this country on a scholarship. Cox further said how he had explained the Party's inability to do anything, especially in view of the fact that the NUM [National Union of Mineworkers] had had discussions with the leaders of the African Mine Workers Union when they had been over here, and they had formed some kind of fraternal association. (It seemed that the man in question was very active in the S. Rhodesian Mine Workers Union). This organisation might sponsor him to WFTU.

WARNING
No action is to be taken on this material without reference to the responsible section, nor may its contents be disclosed outside the Service without permission.

20.

Commander Special Branch
PF 97, 471/B.1.C/PER
Dated: 4th December 1952

JOAN ROSCOE
(Further particulars unknown)
We understand from a delicate source that a woman of this name is apparently living with Doris May Lessing (your 402/50/398 refers) at her address 71, Church Street, London W. 8. We have not been able to identify Roscoe, and would be grateful for your assistance and for any information on her of Security interest that you may be able to provide.
P. B. Ray

21.

PF 97, 471
Name: Lessing
Receipt Date: 19.12.52
Extract from S.B. Report re the Teachers for Peace Organisation mentioning Lessing.

The following information has been obtained from a reliable source regarding the Teachers for Peace Organisation.
This organisation has formed a Sponsoring Committee in Hammersmith under the chairmanship of Lady Barbara Tyrrell (PF 402/44/1415). Some of the committee members are: [blank space]
On 23.11.1952 at the Congregational Hall, Hammersmith, the West London Branch of the Teachers for Peace Organisation held a meeting to give parents its views on peace. The undermentioned persons spoke at the meeting.
[...]
Doris Lessing (PF 402/50/398), who said she recently visited the USSR, as a member of the Authors' World Peace Delegation [...].

22.

Metropolitan Police
Special Branch
Subject: Gottfried Anton Nicolai Lessing
Ref. 402/50/398
19th Day of December 1952

With reference to MI5 letter No. PF 97, 471/B.1.G./
PBR dated 24.11.52. requesting any further informa-
tion this department may be able to provide regarding
the present identity and whereabouts of Gottfried
Anton Nicolai Lessing, subject of Special Branch file
PF/402/50/398:

This man has not come under notice of Special Branch
since the last report on him dated 27th June 1950, and
further discreet enquiries have failed to reveal his
present whereabouts.

When Lessing left his last known address – 30,
Steeles Road, N.W. 3 – in October or November 1950,
he left no forwarding address and all letters arriving
for him [were] re-addressed to Dorothy Schwartz (PF/
402/50/1552) who took over his room. An attempt was
made in August 1951, to obtain Lessing's address from
her by subterfuge. She stated then that Lessing had
gone to Germany and although she could not divulge
his address, she was prepared to re-address any letters sent to him at 30, Steeles Road.

Enquiries now show that Dorothy Schwartz left
30, Steeles Road recently and is said to be living
at 'Oakhurst House, The Ridge, Hastings' (Tele. No.
Baldslow 264).

As far as can be ascertained, Lessing is not in
touch with his former wife Dorothy [sic] May Lessing
of 71, Church St., W. 8., nor has he left any forwarding address at Southern Rhodesia House.

30 Steeles Road is notorious in the neighbourhood as a hot-bed of Communists and does not lend itself to easy enquiry and the landlady, Mrs Dinora Marr (no trace in Special Branch registry) does not appear to be a person who can be trusted.
Submitted.
Chief Inspector

23.

Extract for File No. PF 97, 471
Name: Lessing, Doris May
Receipt Date: 22.12.52

Extract from S. B. report re Rodker, Joan Michel mentioning Lessing, D. M.
With reference to MI5 letter No. PF 97,471/B. I. G./ PBR, dated 4.12.52 asking for this identity of Joan Roscoe, apparently living with Doris May Lessing at 71, Church St., W. 8.

The correct address of Doris May Lessing is 71, Kensington Church Street, W. 8. and there is no Church St. W. 8. Enquiries have failed to trace any woman of the name of Joan Roscoe at this address, but the subject of the MI5 enquiry appears to be identical with Joan Michel Rodker, a secretary and translator, born 1.5.15, an active communist, subject of PF 402/ 49/28 who is said to share a flat with Lessing at the above address.

N. B. Outgoing letter to S. B. filed at 52a in PF 97, 471 Vol. 2.

1953

I.

Extract for File No. PF 97, 471
Name: Lessing, G.
Receipt Date: 17.1.53
Extract from Intercept letter to Mr D. Buckle, 57,
Charlwood Street, London, S.W. 1. from Dorothy
Schwartz, 'Oakhurst', The Ridge, Hastings, Sussex,
mentioning: Lessing, G.

Many thanks for your letter and for the message from
Godfrey [*sic*]. It was nice hearing from him again and
I'm certainly very pleased to hear that he and Ilse
are going to be married. It was a suggestion I made to
both of them separately when I saw them in Berlin in
'51. If you should see either of [or] both of them at
any time, after going through the necessary formula,
please tell them how very glad I am about the news.
　[...]
　By the way, Doris Lessing is coming here on 24th to
meet the local writers' group and speak on her visit
to Russia. I am hoping to address the local Women's
Section of the L. P. on Southern Africa in the not too
distant future. And I'm hoping that you will be able
to speak to an open branch meeting on some aspect of
the Colonies when you have the time and which could
be combined with a little holiday, anyway let me know
when it is convenient.
　[...]

2.

Extract for File No. PF 97, 471
Name: Lessing
Receipt Date: 28.1.53

    o/g call from Maggie to Western 4479 for Doris
Lessing. Maggie wondered if Doris could come next
Saturday, instead of the Saturday after that; Doris
couldn't manage Saturday. Maggie had a chat with
Hymie and finally fixed for Distant to come on Sunday
8th February at about 19.00.
    J. M. Rodker
    71, Church Street, W. 8.

3.

Extract for File No. PF 97, 471
Name: Lessing, Mrs
Receipt Date: 19.3.53
*Extract from BIF Source report re new members of
the Society for Cultural Relations with the USSR
mentioning Lessing, Mrs*

The following are new members of the SCR with the
USSR and joined sometime between February 11th and
March 10th 1953:
    [...]
    Mrs D. Lessing, 71, Church Street, London, W. 8.
Tel. No. Western 4497

4.

Responsible Section B.1.A/MRS
Date and Time of Despatch: 20.4. 53

Visitor with Bob Schwartz
    11.14 They are speaking about Doris Lessing.
Believe she is, or has been ill. Visitor 11. 6 thinks

that of all their writers she is the most promising.
He leaves.

5.

Temple Bar 2151 (Communist Party H. Q.)
Incoming: 21.4.53

Doris Lessing rang Emil Burns and asked if she
could come to see him about something that afternoon.
They arranged finally for the next morning at 9.30
or 10.00.

6.

Temple Bar 2151. (Communist Party H. Q.)
Incoming: 22.4.53

Doris (Lessing??) rang Emil Burns. She said that
the previous day she had a terrific problem in connection with a novel and she thought she would come down
and discuss it [with] Emil. Now she has thought it
over and thinks it would be silly to bother him with
it. She is going to by-pass the particular problem –
it was a question of the Party in the book, but if
she does it in a different way it would be quite un-
necessary to bother Emil. She thanked him and said she
was sorry she had rung up so dramatically.

7.

Temple Bar 2151 (Communist Party H. Q.)
Outgoing: 19.6.53

Jack (Cohen) rang Sam (Aaronovitch) at (Mountview
1885) and asked him to ring Doris Lessing at home,
Western 4479.

8.

Extract for File No. PF 97, 471
Name: Lessing, Doris
Receipt Date: 25.9.53
*Extract from SB Report re People's Books Co-operative
Society Ltd., [mentioning] Lessing, Doris.*

With reference to minute No. 3 on the attached file
asking for a report on the particulars of the People's
Books Co-operative Society Ltd. file with the Registrar
of Friendly Societies:
  The form of application for registration is dated
9.7.53 and signed by seven persons described as members of the Society, and a secretary.
  These are as follows:
  [...]
  6. Doris Lessing, 71, Church St., W. 8. This woman
is the subject of SB file PF 402/50/398 (MI5. PF 97,
491/B.1.G/PBR) where her full address is shown as 71
Kensington Church St., W. 8.

9.

Extract for File No. PF 97, 471
Name: Lessing
Receipt Date: 16.11.53
*Copy of SLO Southern Rhodesia letter re Charles
Mzingeli, mentioning Lessing.*

You may be interested to hear that Doris Lessing (your
PF 97, 471 B1G/PBR of 11.9.52) has sympathised with
Charles Mzingeli because he was refused a passport by
the Southern Rhodesia Government to visit Europe (at
the expense of WFTU Publications Ltd.). She hopes to
have the matter raised by the progressive MPs during
the House of Commons debate on British Guiana.

My OF 1104 dated 8th October 1953, paragraph 3 refers
to Mzingeli's proposed journey. This information was
obtained by local source SWIFT.

1954

I.

Extract for File No. PF 97, 471
Name: Lessing Doris
Receipt Date: 25.2. 54

Extracted from Intercept letter dated 22.2.54 from
John St. John, 591, Finchley Road, N.W.S. (Secretary
of Authors' World Peace Appeal – Communist Penetrated
Organisation, in 1951, and another of AWPA Publications
Panel from 1953–5) to D. M. Ross, 33, Antrim Mansions,
Antrim Road, N.W. 3. Enclosing List of Prospective
Signatures for a circular fostering British China
Friendship, mentioning Doris Lessing.

Sorry to be so long in replying but been fever-
ishly busy with an annual conference. Glad things are
going so well. Here are some addresses:

[...]

Doris Lessing, 71, Church St., Kensington, W. 8.

I think that the above are the most likely ones.
I enclose my own signature – not that it is worth
anything.

John St John

2.

Section and Officer of origin: F.4./HDW
Report Date: 30.3.54
Report

According to a reliable source and well-placed source the leader of the Writers' Group of the British Communist Party is Doris Lessing of 71, Kensington Church Street, W. 8.

3.

Extract for File No. PF 97, 471
Name: Lessing
Receipt Date: 11.6.54
Extract from int. Officers' Minutes British-Soviet Friendship Society Meeting, dated 8.6.54 forwarded to Mr A. Rothstein, 39, Hillway, N. 6. mentioning Lessing, Mrs Doris.

1. Book Club [...]
b. Proposed and agreed we ask the following to come on Managment Committee: Dorris [*sic*] Lessing.

4.

Section and Officer of origin: F.4/HDW
Report Date: 18.6.54

Report
According to a reliable and well-placed source, Doris Lessing of 71, Kensington Church Street, W. 8, has offered her services to the National Cultural Committee of the British Communist Party. She has stated that she is prepared to speak on: 'A Writer looks at the S.U.'

5.

Security Liaison Office
Salisbury
Southern Rhodesia

Our Ref.: PF 86
Your Ref.: ZS 451/X12/2/9
11th June 1954

Doris May Lessing
Will you please refer to your letter dated 28th
May 1954.
    I was interested to hear of the report in *Sunday
Mail* (which I had not spotted) that Mrs Lessing, the
Rhodesian novelist, is now dramatic critic of the
Daily Worker.
    I enclose a short note on her background.
    Yours,
    Security Liaison Officer,
    Central Africa,
    (B. M. De Quehen)

J. C. Day, Esq.
Assistant Commissioner,
CID & Special Branch,
Box 203
Lusaka

6.

London Airport
Metropolitan Police (Special Branch)
18th day of June 1954
Subject: Doris May Lessing

Mrs Doris May Lessing, British, born in Kermanshaw, Persia, on 22.10.19 was among the passengers arriving at this airport from Paris at 10. 30 p.m. today. She appeared to be unaccompanied, and was in possession of British passport, No. 1553 issued London 9.11.51, in which she is described as a 'Writer'.

It was noticed that her passport contained several 1952 visas for 'Iron Curtain' countries.

A discreet search of her baggage by H. M. Customs revealed nothing of interest to Special Branch.

Constable

[signature illegible]

7.

Extract for File No. PF 97, 471
Name: Lessing
Receipt Date: 28.6.54
Extract from Intercepted Minutes of National Council Meeting, held on 20th June 1954 at 14, Kensington Square, W. 8 of the British Soviet Friendship Society, 36, Spenser Street, E.C.1, mentioning Lessing.

9. The Book Club:

A Management Committee of the Russia Today was then elected as follows, it being understood that on all questions relating to the Club final authority rests with the BSFS and that this should be expressed in an appropriately worded Constitution for the Book Club.

Miss Barbour, Miss Lessing, Messers Lindsay, Sloan, Creighton, Fagan, Sutherland (the foregoing are the present Selection Committee); Messers Brian Pearce, James Mortimer, Dave Michaelson, Tom Russell, Mrs Y. Kapp, Misses Margaret Mynatt, Doris Lessing, Bessie Bleacher (as Secretary).

8.

Extract for: PF 97, 471
Lessing, Doris
Commander,
Special Branch
17th August 1954

The National Council of the British Soviet Friendship
Society has recently appointed a Management Committee
for the Russia Today Book Club. This Committee is
responsible to the National Council of the British
Soviet Friendship Society for the general administration of the Book Club, and for the choice of books to
be distributed. Members of the Club are as follows:
   [...]
   Lessing, Doris
   P. Commings

9.

Temple Bar 2151 (Communist Party H.Q.)
11 Sep. 1954

Doris Lessing rang Sam Aaronovitch. She wanted to buy
a cheap house and wondered if Sam knew a lawyer who
could help her. Sam said Chris Vowles in Hampstead
might help.

10.

Extract for File No. PF 97, 471
Name: Lessing
Original in File No. PF 135,351 Tikhonov
Receipt Date: 19.12.54

Copy of telegram from British Embassy, Moscow to P.U.S.D. Foreign Office re Soviet Writers' Congress, mentioning Doris Lessing.
Restricted.
From Moscow to Foreign Office
D.4.06.p.m. December 23, 1954

In his report to Soviet Writers' Congress yesterday on the modern progressive literature of the world N. S. Tikhonov named the following British writers: Sean O'Casey, Alfred Coppard, James Aldridge, Jack Lindsay, Gwynn Thomas, Doris Lessing. BBC on this unrepresentative character might be appropriate.

1955 (1)

I.

Section and Officer of origin: F.4/MK
Report No. 13, 602
Typing Date: 18.1. 55

Report
It is understood that Doris Lessing, the Authoress, is a Party member.

2.

Section and Officer of origin: F.4/MK
Report No. 13, 652
Typing Date: [illegible]

Report

It is reported that Doris Lessing, 58, Warwick Road,
S.W. 5 was a member of the Holland Park C.P. at
15.1.55.
    [ ]
    We have a membership card for her up to 1953.

3.

Temple Bar 2151 (Communist Party H.Q.)
Outgoing: 1.2.55

To Lawrence & Wishart. Sam Aaronovitch from Golly.
    Golly was ringing for Emile (Burns) who wanted
Doris Lessing's address. It was:
58, Warwick Road, S.W. 5.
    She was not in the telephone book as she had only
recently moved to this address. She was Mrs Lessing,
not Miss. There was no Mr Lessing 'around'.

4.

CONFIDENTIAL
Parliament Street, B.O.
London, S.W. 1.
Commander, S.B.,
Scotland Yard.
Date 19.2.55

Holland Ward (Kensington) branch
Name: Lessing, Mrs Doris May
Address: 1955: 58, Warwick Road, Earls Court, S.W. 5
Security Information. 1955: Member of Holland Park
(Kensington) branch of the Communist Party.

5.

Extract for: PF 97, 471
Name: Doris Lessing
Dated: 13.4.55

Precis
Included in the list (forwarded by F.4) of subscribers
to *Preview*, Vol. II, No. 6 for March 1955 – the
journal of the Film Panel, Author World Peace Appeal
(Communist penetrated organisation) is:
Doris Lessing, 71, Church Street, W. 8.

6.

South African Police
Headquarters
Pretoria
13th June 1955

Dear Sir,
Robert Knox Cope @ Jack Cope
Born: 3.6. 1913, in South Africa
Address: 'Trinity Hall', Fourth Beach, Clifton, Cape
    Information has been received from a reliable source
that a certain 'Dos' of 58, Warwick Road, London,
S.W.5, is in touch with the above named, a well known
South African Communist, who has been listed as such
by the Liquidator appointed in terms of the Suppression
of Communist Act *[sic]*, 1950.
    According to our source 'Dos' a former theatre
critic of the *Daily Worker*, intends visiting Rhodesia
and probably the Union of South Africa in the near
future.
    Any information which you may be able to furnish us
concerning this person, would be greatly appreciated.
    Yours sincerely,
    for The Commissioner of the South African Police
    [signature illegible]

The Director General
Box No. 500,
Parliament Street B.O.
London, S.W.1.

7.

PF 97,471
18th July 1955

Dear General Rademeyer,
    Please refer to your letter dated 13th June 1955
regarding 'Doris', 58, Warwick Road, London, S.W. 5,
who is reported to be in touch with Robert Knox Cope
@ Jack Cope.
    We have now identified this person as Mrs Doris May
Lessing, British Subject, born 22nd October 1919, at
Kermanshah, Persia, a writer, who is known to us as an
active Communist. She lived in Southern Rhodesia until
1949 where she came to notice in connection with her
Communist sympathies; she was reported to be a member
of the Rhodesian Friends of the Soviet Union and to
have distributed copies of *Guardian* in Salisbury.
    Her second husband, Gottfried Anton Nicolai Lessing,
a naturalised British subject, born 14th December 1914,
in Leningrad, Russia, from whom she is now divorced,
also come to our notice in a Communist context. He was
mentioned in our PF 73,415/B.1.g/ [illegible], dated
24th April 1951, as a contact of Ilse Dadoo (Contacts
in Europe, number 3). Mr Lessing was last reported to
be living at Taubenstrasse 1-2, Berlin, W. 8.
    Yours sincerely
    Director General
    [signature illegible]

Major General C. I. Rademeyer
Commissioner of South African Police
P.O. Box 1895
Pretoria, South Africa

8.

PF 97, 471/E.2/JP
18th July 1955
To: SLO Central Africa
From: Head Office

Reference the attached letter. Mr Lessing was sub-ject of your PF 86 dated 15th November 1953, and Mrs Lessing was the subject of your PF 86 dated 11th June 1954, to Special Branch, Lusaka, copied to us.

Robert Cope referred to is a well known South African Communist listed by the Liquidator. The South African Police report that Mrs Lessing intends vis-iting Rhodesia and probably South Africa in the near future.

A delicate and reliable source known to you has reported that Mrs Lessing joined the British Communist Party in 1952. This is passed to you for information *only,* in view of the previous doubt as to the extent of her sympathies (see our letter of 11th September 1952).

Photo 1. Gottfried Lessing and his son, Peter

Photo 2. Doris Lessing and her son, Peter

Photo 3. Doris, Gottfried and Peter

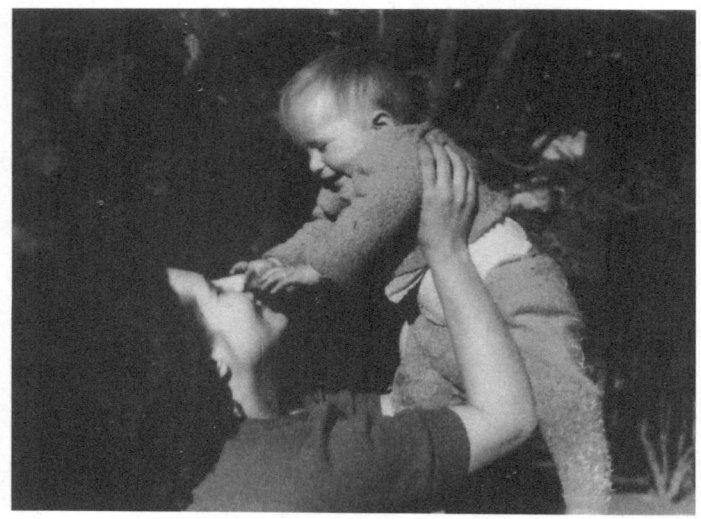

Photo 4. Doris and Peter

Photo 5. Doris and Peter

Photo 6. Gottfried Anton Nicolai Lessing

Visits to 'Central Africa' and their Aftermath

1955 (2)

9.

Extract for File No. PF 97,471
Name: Lessing, Doris
Date of Delivery: 19.7.55

Cox speaking to Visitor (possibly Vella) Pillay
    12.52 Cox then spoke for a moment or two about the situation, and then told V. that Doris Lessing and Paul?Hobart [*sic*], the?artist [*sic*], were probably going to S. Africa for the NEWS CHRONICAL (*sic*). It seemed that Doris Lessing had asked for the names of comrades with whom she might get in touch. Cox thought this was a bit ticklish and asked V.'s advice. Cox told V. that he proposed to give her the name of Ray Alexander, who, in any case, held a public position, but he wanted to know if he should tell her about the others, Bram (Fisher) and Berrange.
    V. then spoke almost inaudibly for a minute or two, making reference to?Peter [*sic*],? Watson [*sic*],?Brenda Watts [*sic*]. They seemed to agree not to tell 'her' to 'approach Bram'. Cox said that 'she' had had a talk with Simon? [*sic*] not so much about S. Africa as about Rhodesia, because Charles Mzingeli and she had met? [*sic*] here.

WARNING
No action is to be taken on this material without reference to the responsible section, nor may its

*contents be disclosed outside the Service without
permission.*

10.

Extract for File No. PF 97, 471
Name: Lessing
Date of contents: 20.7.55

Zukas (to Cox) said something about 'something from
South Africa' and Cox said that Vella (Pillay) was
supposed to enquire but he didn't know whether he had
done anything about it yet. Cox told Zukas he had
seen Doris Lessing last week at Oakhurst and she had
said she had been going to South Africa for the *News
Chronicle* but this had been called off. Zukas said he
had thought it couldn't be true that she was going.

11.

[no date]
Elt Doris Lessing c/o Daily Worker London EC1

Airmail your play to me Care Peace Committee Moscow
View Transaction BT [*sic*] Monica AR

12.

30 Aug. 1955

N809 YM54 MOSCOW 20 9 2110 ETAT URSSGOVT
DORIS LESSING 71 KENSINGTON CHURCH STREET LONDON NW 8
WE ARE IMPATIENTLY WAITING FOR PROMISED ARTICLE EDITOR
IN CHIEF LITERARY GAZETTE RYURIKOV AR

13.

21st September 1955
Confidential
To the Immigration Officer

Doris May Lessing (Mrs)
Born: 22.10.19 Kermanshah, Persia
Nationality: British. Formerly German
Last known address: 58, Warwick Road, Earls Court,
London, S. W. 5
Profession: Authoress
Documents: Passport 1553 issued London 9.11.51
A communist who is likely to visit Africa in the near
future.
Discreetly obtain United Kingdom address and particu-
lars of Foreign visas and documents of interest, and
telephone arrival or departure to MI5.
  C. P. J. Ruck
  H.M. Chief Inspector

14.

PFB 187
30th September 1955
To: SLO Central Africa

Mrs Doris May Lessing
1. Local delicate source indicates that on 18th
September, the above named contacted Charles Mzingeli
of Salisbury and informed him that Simon Zukas's address is: 1, Goodwood House, Park Court, Lowrie Perk
Road, S.E. 26. (This is the same address as the one
given by your Head Office in their G.P. 1048/g.2/JP of
9th September 1955.) She had telephoned Zukas and told
him about Mzingeli's problem (what the problem is we
do not know). Zukas apparently told her that Fenner
Brockway is a man who tries to control movements of

this sort and to make them respectable. He says that there are several friends in this movement with political views the same as his own and Charles Mzingeli is advised to support it.

2. Doris Lessing says that one 'Basil' agrees with this view. 'Basil' apparently is not in England at present but in Morocco, but Doris Lessing is in touch with his wife who is in England.

3. Some one named 'Dorothy' is said to be in Hastings and rather out of touch with things.

4. Doris Lessing also says that Fenner Brockway's organisation may easily play a very progressive role depending on pressure from those inside it. (Comment: this may possibly refer to the Communist penetration of the Movement for Colonial Freedom. We should welcome your views on this point.)

5. Charles Mzingeli is advised to write to Simon Zukas about all this because he is very well informed on everything that goes on. There is no indication that Doris Lessing will visit Rhodesia in the near future but she looks forward to seeing Mzingeli in London some time. Your Head Office letter PF 97,471 of 18th July 1955 refers and it is noted that Mrs Lessing joined the British Communist Party in 1952 and is described as an active Communist. She is of course the novelist and author of 'Rustling Grass' [sic] and other novels concerning Rhodesian life.

6. We should be most interested to hear your Head Office views on this intelligence.

B. M. de Quehen
Director, FISB

15.

PFB 187
4th October 1955
To: SLO Central Africa

Further to my letter PFB. 187 of 30th September 1955,
paragraph 2, Basil is id/w Basil Davidson; paragraph
3, 'Dorothy' may be Dorothy Schwartz, perhaps?

I omitted in my 'scrambled' version to say 'Peter
and friends' of Mzingeli had returned his greetings.
'Peter' may perhaps be identical with the Kenya African
Peter Koinange.

I would welcome your comments.

B. M. de Quehen,

Director, FISB

16.

Extract for: PF 97, 471
Name: Doris Lessing
Dated: 19.10.55
*Extract from F4 Source Report enclosing list of members
(1955) of the Writers' Group of the Communist Party.*

Among those mentioned is.
Doris Lessing, 58, Warwick Road, S.W. 5.

Comments by Section of Origin.
Reliable source who obtained this list in very delicate circumstances which are on record on F.4. files.

Comments by Consumer Section.
Thank you. This is extremely valuable.

Note:
Over 90% of the members of the C. P. Writers' Group
are also normal card-holding members. According to a
well-placed source, however, there are a few members
of the Group who for private reasons are not full Party
members, and others who are brought along to meetings
of the Writers' Group in the hope that they may be
attracted into the Party. This appears to be confirmed
by our own records, which show that a number of these

listed as members of the Group were previously known
to us only as communist sympathisers; while some are
N.T. Membership of the C. P. Writers' Group, [and]
unless confirmed by other evidence of Party membership
should, in making security assessments, usually be
classed as 'strong communist sympathisers'.

17.

November 1955
*Comment on FISB reports (reference PFB 187) of 30th
September and 4th October 1955.*

    Paragraph 1.
A delicate and reliable source in this country has
confirmed that Mrs Lessing was in touch with Simon
Zukas during September in connection with a query received from Mzingeli. This source did not explain the
details of the problem. We can confirm that Zukas's
present address is 1, Goodwood House, Park Court,
[illegible] Park Road, London, S.E. 26.
    Paragraph 2.
'Basil' is doubtless Basil Davidson who recently
visited Morocco on behalf of the *Daily Herald*.
    Paragraph 3.
'Dorothy' is Dorothy Schwartz, part owner of
'Oakhurst', The Ridge, Hastings, a Communist run
guest-house.
    Paragraph 4.
The organisation is almost certainly The Movement for
Colonial Freedom and we imagine that Charles Mzingeli
had received notification of the World Conference for
Colonial Liberation which was held at Margate November
5th-7th. He was no doubt uncertain as to how much
support he should give the organisation and was en-
quiring through Doris Lessing for Zukas's views upon
it. (Compare last two sentences of your paragraph 1).

    Note.
In addition to the comments given above, we notice
with interest Mzingeli got in touch with Lessing and
not with Zukas direct. It is significant that although Mzingeli visited Zukas's home when in the
United Kingdom earlier in the year he had apparently
failed to take note of, or had lost, Zukas's address
and that he does not seem to have been given details
of any more clandestine method of getting in touch
with Zukas.

1956 (1)

I.

Metropolitan Police
Special Branch
RF 402/50/398
MI5. PF 97, 471
28th day of January 1956

The following information was obtained from Erich
George Kuehne or Kuhne, Czech, of 58, Warwick Road,
S.W. 5 (ground and basement flat), who was the subject
of my report of 17th January 1956, in connection with
his wife's application for a certificate of naturalisation (350/55/488), and who is very anti-Communist.
    Mrs Lessing, who occupies the two top floors at 58,
Warwick Road, is a Communist. Her flat is frequently
visited by persons of various nationality, including
Americans, Indians, Chinese and Negroes. Mrs Lessing
is not always at home when these visits take place,
as she appears to be away frequently from the address.
Some of the visitors seem to stay at the flat for days
at a time and some of the visits are made by apparently unmarried couples. A lot of correspondence is

received at the flat for Mrs Lessing and the persons with whom she associates. It is possible that the flat is being used for immoral practices.

Mrs Lessing is Doris May or Dorothy Lessing, nee Taylor, formerly Wisdom, who is known to Special Branch (RF 402/50/398) and MI5 (PF 97, 471) as a Communist. Her name is in the British Suspect Index. There is no other adverse trace of her in Metropolitan Police records.

Kensington CID have been informed about the alleged immoral practices in Lessing's flat, and arrangements will be made by them to have the premises kept under observation, when possible. The address has not previously come to their notice.

Submitted.

Sergeant.

Superintendent.

Chief Superintendent

2.

Extract for File No. PF 97, 471
Name: Lessing
Receipt Date: 3.3. 56

From July 4th to 8th will take place in Paris the 'European Gathering of Young Women for Peace and Happiness'. The very title of this Gathering gives the essential idea of what it will be. [...].

The World Federation of Democratic Youth took the initiative of this Gathering. It called upon all internationals and national organisations to contribute to its preparations and to participate in it.

An International Sponsoring Committee for the Gathering is being formed. Personalities – who will be more numerous tomorrow – of several countries have enthusiastically accepted to support the Gathering. Among others, we quote:

from Great Britain:
    Mrs Doris Lessing, writer,
    Dr Monica Felton, President of the British Assembly
of Women.

3.

Section and Officer of origin: F.4/ Arts
Typing Date: 6.3.56

Report
Doris Lessing, telephone number FRE: 4097, is a member
of the Communist Party who has been described as 'a
literary ace in the Party'.

4.

Extract for File No. PF 97, 471
Name: Lessing
Receipt Date: 28.3.56
*Copy of T/C on King Street Call Box. Desmond Buckle
to Dick Greenfield.*

King Street Call Box.
Outgoing 27.3.56
Hounslow 4822

Desmond Buckle rang Dick Greenfield and said he had
been asked to get in touch with him in connection
with a project they had of sending Paul Hogarth to
South Africa. Did Dick know about it? They had been
collecting some money for his expenses and so on but
so far they had not got all that they had wanted,
there was the fare and everything else and he had
been asked to approach Greenfield to see if he would
make a donation to the thing. They wanted to set off

with Doris Lessing on Thursday morning. They had got his ticket all right but they had not got enough for the customs requirements and so forth and there was only to-day and tomorrow. [...]

5.

TELEGRAM FOR DESPATCH
To: SLO Central Africa
Office File No. PF 97, 471
Date: 29 March 1956

1. Subject Doris May Lessing, your PF 86, FISB's PFB. 187. Subject left London Airport for Lusaka at 0830 hours on 29 March by Flight S.A. 211.
2. Reported to be visiting Nyasaland and Southern Rhodesia as well.
3. Land states she is likely to attempt to make contacts for future Party use, although main reason for trip probably concerned with writing.
4. Lessing accompanied by Paul Hogarth, free-lance artist and long standing member of BCP.

6.

Metropolitan Police
Special Branch
29th day of March 1956

In confirmation of a telephone message to Chief Superintendent, for transmission to MI5 at 8.40 a.m. today:
    Doris May Lessing, a writer, born 22.10.19, in possession of British Passport No. 242961 issued London on 8.3.56 subject of Home Office British Suspect Index Circular No. BS10127, left this airport for Lusaka at 8.30 a.m. today on flight S.A. 211.

She was accompanied by Arthur Paul Hogarth, an artist, born 4.10.17, in possession of British Passport No. 246356 issued London on 12.3.56.

Customs examination of their baggage failed to reveal anything of interest to Special Branch.

Submitted.

Constable.

Inspector.

Chief Superintendent.

7.

TELEGRAM RECEIVED
From: SLO Central Africa
File No. PF 97, 471
Date of Origin: 4.4.56

1. Reference your telegram DS/5033 of 29th March which we much regret was not sent Philosopher.

2. Please cable all available information on Hogarth and advise as to whether local authorities should deem him prohibited immigrant.

3. Local authorities have deemed Lessing prohibited immigrant but (?she) will be permitted to remain in Southern Rhodesia on temporary permit for one month. As she was declared P.I. without reference to SLO are your sources likely to be compromised?

8.

TELEGRAM FOR DESPATCH
To: SLO Central Africa
Office File No. PF 97, 471
Date: 5 April 1956

1. Much regret delay in our DS 5033 due to unfore-
seen time-lag between leaving E2 and being transmitted.
    2. Little to add on Hogarth. Member of BCP since
1936 and well known free-lance artist. No information
about purpose of trip but possibly associating with
Lessing on book as illustrator. Presumably danger that
if Lessing unable to carry out programme because of
limited time, Hogarth may remain and take over subversive contacts.
    3. No prejudice to source involved in declaring
Lessing a P.I.[1]

9.

Security Liaison Office
Salisbury,
Southern Rhodesia
6th April 1956
To: Head Office

    1. Will you please refer to your telegram DS/5035
of 5th April and earlier telegrams concerning the
visit of Doris Lessing and Paul Hogarth.
    2. These two flew to Johannesburg on 4th April, and
I warned the South African Police of their coming.
Doris Lessing was returned to Rhodesia on the next
aircraft without any explanation having been given to
her by the South African authorities. Paul Hogarth has
not returned and presumably still remains in the Union.
    3. Doris Lessing was very upset by all this, and
from the usual very delicate source we learn that she
has written to Mr and Mrs Zukas at 1, Goodwood House,
Park Court, Lowrie Park Road, S.E. 26, and asking them
to pass to 'Desmond' (presumably Desmond Buckle) advanced notice of what had happened to her. I have not
yet seen the information which she passed, but I am

1   PI = Prohibited Immigrant.

informed that it is very precise and indicates that the pair of them are out here to do a specific job of work which confirms your telegram DS/5033 of 29th March, paragraph 3.

4. Doris Lessing has been permitted to remain here on temporary permit which expires in about three weeks' time; but if her activities come to adverse notice, the Federal Immigration authorities reserve the right to send her back to the United Kingdom – since she has already been deemed as P.I.

Security Liaison Officer,
Central Africa,
(B. M. de Quehen)

10.

Security Liaison Office
Salisbury,
Southern Rhodesia
11th April 1956
To: Head office

Mrs Doris Lessing
The following telegram was phoned from the house of Carol Zelter by Mrs Doris Lessing at 0850 on 5th April.

Rodker, 71, Church Street, London, S.W. 5.

Refused permission to enter Union 4th April. Declared Prohibited Immigrant. Please release Reuters. Try Freeman Hopkinson Jones. As usual my love you and everybody. All O. K. Doris.

We have a trace of a Mrs Joan Rodker who was the assistant secretary of the Kensington Peace Group and appears in the list of members of the South African Peace Group which you sent us under cover of your O.F.747/B.i.g/CPCdeW dated 7th March 1952, addressed to the South African Police. Presumably these people are identical and we should be glad to know whether you have additional information concerning Mrs Joan Rodker.

    Security Liaison Officer,
    Central Africa,
    (B. M. de Quehen)

II.

Extract for File No. PF 218, 584; PF 97,471
Name: Lindsay, Jack; Lessing, Doris
Receipt Date. 28.4.56
Original from: T/C on Temple Bar 2151
Dated: 25.4.56

Joan Carrit to Emil Burns.
Joan wanted to know if Emil could recommend anyone to open a discussion in her Children's Committee, about the importance of literature in the battle of ideas.
    Emil suggested:
Jack Lindsay, Castle Hedingham, Halstead, Essex.
Doris Lessing, 58, Warwick Road, S.W. 5.

12.

PFB 187
30th April 1956
To: *Private Secretary to the Prime Minister*

Doris Lessing
Paul Hogarth
    These two Communists are still in or around Salisbury, Doris Lessing having visited Bulawayo and Gwelo. They are using Carol Nathan Zelter's fawn Consul, Number S. 33135 and are taking a great deal of evasive action and abnormal security precautions

to shake off surveillance. In fact, at the time of writing, CID have lost track of them but hope to pick them up later in the day.

While in Bulawajo, Doris Lessing stayed with Francis Ivor Williams and in Gwelo with the Loveridges. In Salisbury she and Hogarth are living at the Zelter's house in Lawson Avenue where they have seen a great deal of another local Communist, Harry Chimovitz. They propose in the near future to visit Kariba, Northern Rhodesia, and Nyasaland. (The Northern Territories have been alerted.)

The difficulties of keeping these very alert people under surveillance emphasises the need for a properly equipped Special Branch. Moreover, even though the CID are in reasonable touch with the movements of these people, it is not really known what mischief they are up to. It is learned confidentially that SRG have 'agreed in principle' to the Commissioner's request for more Europeans and Africans to be employed solely on security duties. However, even if there are no further hitches it will be some time before his recommendations can be implemented. The European wastage in the CID is considerable and the training of Special Branch officers is a long process.

A more detailed report of the movements of Doris Lessing and Paul Hogarth will be submitted when they leave the Federation. Hogarth is understood to be returning to the United Kingdom on the 18th May and Doris Lessing on the 24th May.

B. M. de Quehen
Director, FISB

13.

PFB 187
12th May 1956
To: SLO Central Office

We have received a report that Wilfred Gordon McDonald Partridge, who was born in Australia on 25.8.1912, may have been contacted by Mrs Doris Lessing while she was staying with Francis Ivor Williams in Bulawayo. Partridge, who is the Principal of the London Missionary Society School at Hope Fountain near Bulawayo, is known to have been connected with the Inter-Racial Club in Bulawayo for several years and to be a contact of Williams. It is perhaps not without significance that it was from Hope Fountain Mission that the South African Communist teacher and research worker, John Ardene Rex, was deported in 1949. We should be grateful to know whether your Head Office and Australia have any trace of Partridge.

It has also been reported that Mrs Lessing has stated, at a public meeting that she attended, that she might come back to Rhodesia for permanent residence after she has written her book on the Federation. If after her return to the United Kingdom, you receive any indications that she might come back to Rhodesia permanently, we should be glad [to hear] about it so that the Immigration Authorities here can enforce the order deeming her a prohibited immigrant to the Federation, before she starts her journey.

B. M. de Quehen
Director, FISB

14.

PFB 187
16th May 1956

Mrs Doris May Lessing
Activities in Rhodesia from 30th March – 25th April 1956

1. Since the arrival of Mrs Lessing and her friend Paul Hogarth, who is a free-lance artist and a member of the British Communist Party, in the Federation, the following information has been reported.

2. A delicate source reveals that Mrs Lessing has been in touch with the *Daily Herald* and has sent them a short statement of the reason why she was banned from the Union of South Africa; she has also been in communication with Mrs Joan Rodker, a South African now living in London, who is the Assistant Secretary of the Kensington Peace Group.

3. It has been established that that Mrs Lessing and Paul Hogarth visited Umtali during the Easter weekend in the company of Carol Nathan Zelter, with whom they had been staying in Salisbury, and Marjorie Chisnall. At this stage it must be explained that from the security point of view nothing is recorded here or in the United Kingdom to the detriment of Miss Chisnall, who is an LCC Headmistress. She was staying with the Zelters at the time and has since returned to London. On the other hand, Zelter and his wife, Dorothy, who is now in England, have a Communist background which goes back to the early days of the last war. Zelter is a Rumanian and runs an agency in Salisbury.

4. The local Communists also visited the Eastern Districts during the Easter weekend. They were Francis Ivor Williams, who is looked upon by The British Communist Party as their most important contact in Central Africa; he is known to be very security conscious and tries to avoid undue attention; and Harry Chinowitz of Avondale, Sailsbury, who is a civil engineer of Russian/Jewish parents; he was active in the Rhodesia Study Group at Cape Town University during the time that Simon Ber Zukas resided there. Chimowitz is now employed as Roads Department engineer in the Sinoia district and his wife, Margorie, also holds Communist views. Williams is also a civil servant and is employed as a shorthand writer in the Magistrates Court, Bulawayo; he is the secretary of the Matabeleland Branch of the Civil Service Association. The communication between these two persons, arranging their holiday weekend were conducted in a clandestine manner and Williams is known to have used a false name.

5. Williams and Chimowitz, and Chimowitz's family, are believed to have visited St Faith's Mission, Rusapo, during the weekend although it has not been definitely proved. It was known that Chimowitz planned to stay with Ralph Gordon Ibbott, of the Mission staff, sometimes during the year. Ibbott has a certain security background. Williams/Chimowitz, however, are known to have camped near the Mission on a farm, Lesape Dale [illegible]. They were joined there by Anthony Cullen Bowles who has recently resigned from the Department of Justice; he is not a substantial risk to security but he is known to be a contact of Williams.

6. It is not known whether the two parties met during the Easter weekend although there was, subsequently, evidence of frequent contact between them all.

7. Another character, holding dubious political views, went to Umtali during the Easter weekend and that was Frederick Karl Baraf, a Government Health Inspector. This man was born in Vienna in 1907 and arrived in Southern Rhodesia as a refugee in 1938. He has since become naturalized. He is a close associate of the Zelters, and was there frequently with Mrs Lessing. He is a man well-versed in Russian affairs and has an unmistakable sympathy for Communism.

8. It is also known that some members of the Lessing/Zelter party were in touch with two members of the Native Education Department of Southern Rhodesia, namely Charles Michael Drury and Frederick Gerald Gardener, both of Umtali. Both are friends of Baraf. Drury was born in London about 1911 and came to Southern Rhodesia in 1938. He held a teaching post at Gatooma and later at Prince Edward School. Early in 1955 he was President of the Southern Rhodesia Teachers' Association and the same year was appointed head of the Government African Teacher Training School in Umtali. Gardener was born in London in 1903 and came to Southern Rhodesia to a teaching post at Milton School, Bulawayo. He was transferred to Prince Edward School in 1937 and ten years later was appointed Inspector of African Schools. Neither of these two

are reported to have been members of the BCP, although they have, since their residence in Southern Rhodesia, proclaimed extremist views. In 1953, the Police received a report based on information from a hitherto reliable source that Drury, Gardener and a colleague Loveridge (who is referred to later in this report) were 'self-avowed Communists who made no effort to hide their Leftist tendencies'.

9. On her return to Salisbury from Umtali, Mrs Lessing again stayed at the Zelters' house. Another guest at that time was John Richard Gray, who is visiting the Federation doing research work for Chatham House. Soon afterwards Mrs Lessing and Paul Hogarth flew to the Union of South Africa where her fears that she might not be allowed to enter the Union were well founded. She was, indeed, refused entry and was declared a prohibited immigrant, returning to Salisbury the same day. Hogarth was allowed to remain in the Union.

10. After her removal from the Union, Mrs Lessing said that she would now concentrate on the Federation where 'things are very interesting'. She then gave out that she was collecting material for another book (it transpired later that this was to be a book on the political and economic aspects of the Federation which will probably be written with a marked anti-Federation bias). She has also said that she will be writing articles for the *Tribune, New Statesman* and *Nation, News Chronicle,* and the *Manchester Guardian.* In addition to these literary activities, it is also reported from a particularly delicate source, that she is likely to make contacts in the Federation for future Party use. This has later proved to be the case.

11. Following a lunch party given at the Zelters house which was attended by Mr and Mrs Charles Mzingeli and, it is believed, Baraf, Mrs Lessing went to Gwelo to stay with Loveridges. Frederick George Loveridge, her Gwelo host, was born in Southern Rhodesia in 1911. He is an Inspector in the Native Education Department at Gwelo, having previously been at Plumtreo School

and the Harari African School. His wife, Phyllis
Monica Loveridge, nee Akers, has a particularly militant Communist Background. She joined the BCP in 1936
and was propaganda secretary of the Hounslow Branch,
before coming to Southern Rhodesia in 1938. It is not
known what transpired between Mrs Lessing and the
Loveridges.

12. After that she went to Bulawayo where she stayed
with Francis Ivor Williams. On the second afternoon
of the Bulawayo visit she went to see Mrs Owen Gibbon
Coleman, a qualified teacher of dramatic art and who
was, up to a month ago, teaching at the Founders
Coloured School, Barham Green, Bulawayo. A number of
Inflammatory statements have been attributed to Mrs
Coleman who is in her 66th year. She has never been
reported as having been a member of the BCP. She has,
however, a daughter in England who shares her mother's
advanced views on inter-racialism. Mrs Lessing accompanied by Williams met a number of leading Africans
during her Bulawayo visit. She interviewed a number
of the Bulawayo City African Administration Department
saying that she would like a job in that department
if possible so that she could live among the Africans
and thus collect first-hand material for her book. This
proposition was not encouraged.

13. In discussions in Bulawayo, Mrs Lessing professed to Communist Party membership without trying to
push the Party line. She said that the Party could do
no more than is being done in the African development
field but that the Party would quicken the progress on
the social side and would soon dispense with all colour
barriers. She professed loyalty to the Commonwealth
saying that half the world was Communist and that ad-
herents now have no need to look to the Soviets for
a lead. Communist progress would be bloodless and
gradual. She said that she had been in China where
she saw tremendous enthusiasm – a feature lacking in
Africans. A visit was also paid to the Alpha Evening
School, at the Lobengula School, and to the Hope
Fountain Mission, the principal of which is Wilfred

Gordon McDonald Partridge, an Australian against whom there are no security traces. It may be pointed out that it was from this Mission that the South African Communist teacher, John Ardene Rex, was deported in 1949. The following is a list of the Africans whom Mrs Lessing appears to have met during her visit to Bulawayo:

Rollek Bango.

Bradford Phiri, President of the Matabeleland Branch of the Nyasaland African Congress.

Cuthbert Sinyangae [illegible], a Northern Rhodesian African who is Vice Chairman of the Bulawayo Branch of the N.R. African Congress.

Keziyasi [?] Portipolio, a Northern Rhodesian African and secretary of the Bulamayo Branch of the Northern Rhodesian African Congress.

14. On the 23rd April, Mrs Lessing left Bulawayo and visited Gwelo again. She had dinner with Dr William Bear Soswab, an American Ford Foundation Research worker whose headquarters in Southern Rhodesia are at Gwelo. She also visited the Senka African Village. She arrived back in Salisbury a few hours before her companion, Hogarth, arrived by air from the Union.

15. The foregoing information indicates the interest which is being taken by Mrs Lessing, who must, we think, be regarded as on a reconnaisance for the BCP in the field of African education. It is learnt that the Prime Minister of Southern Rhodesia has been distressed to note the number of Communist sympathisers who appear to have found refuge in the Native Education Department. It certainly postulates the need for very careful vetting of applicants for teaching posts within the Federation.

16. This is an interim report. Mrs Lessing's other activities in Salisbury and in Northern Rhodesia will be submitted later.

15.

R.E.C. Broadbent, Esq.
c/o Kenya Secretariat,
Nairobi, Kenya
28 May 1956
To: Head Office (2)
SLO Central Africa
PF 86

Doris Lessing and Paul Hogarth
With reference to SLO East Africa's compliment slip
of 4 May forwarding an FISB report, and his telegram
CA/49 to London SLO/39 to Nairobi dated 14 May, some
attention was paid to these persons when they tran-
sited Nairobi on 18 May. They contacted nobody during
their brief stay at Eastleigh Airport. On the plane
from Livingstone they were seen to be busy writing
all the time, but covered up the pages when anyone
passed by.
    R.E.C. Broadbent,
    SLO East Africa

16.

PF 97, 471/E.2/KCT
30 May 1956
SLO Central Africa

    1. Please refer to your telegram CA/50 dated 15
May 1956.
    2. Lessing and Hogarth arrived at London Airport
on 19 May 1956. We noted in your telegram that they
had with them a package of photographs and a large
black note-book containing Rhodesian material. The
possibility of obtaining access to this note-book was
considered in some detail here and it was reluctantly

decided that it would be impossible for us to look in the note-book without arousing Mrs Lessing's suspicions. We were conscious of the fact that she would be on the alert for any sign of tampering with her baggage, in view of her recent article in the *New Statesman* where she accused MI5 of telling the South Africans of her trip.

3. It was consequently decided that we should not ask the Customs Authorities to pay any special attention to Lessing's property and a discreet examination was all that could be made, revealing nothing of security interest.

4. I am sorry that we are unable to comply with your request in this instance but I am sure you will appreciate the reasons for our inability to do so.

17.

PFB 187
4th June 1956

Mrs Doris Lessing in Northern Rhodesia
1. Mrs Lessing in a meeting with Congress leaders of Northern Rhodesia and Nyasaland in Salisbury, before she visited Northern Rhodesia, said that her visit to Central Africa was chiefly made to determine African opinion towards Federation; she also discussed other contentious subjects with them such as:
a) The withdrawal of African labour from Kariba and Shire projects in protest against Federation.
b) Common African policy within the Federation and African franchise.
c) The proposed evacuation and resettlement of Africans living near Kariba.
We know from a secret source that Mrs Lessing was also making contacts for future Communist Party use.
2. Mrs Lessing travelled by air to Ndola on the 7th May 1956, from Salisbury and then went to Kitwe

where she stayed at the Nkana Hotel. She met a number of European and African trade union officials and was the guest of the Rhokana Corporation for lunch with the General Manager Mr O. B. Bennett; she was also taken over the mine and the African Township.

3. Mrs Lessing told her friends in Northern Rhodesia that she was going to write a book about the Federation which would be a kind of political survey. She had gleaned her material from a wide circle of contacts from all walks of life. She had had an interview with the Prime Minister of Southern Rhodesia who had told her (so she said) that she would not be allowed to go to Northern Rhodesia. Later she saw Lord Malvern, who, she said, had also forbidden her to go North, but she had argued with him asking what trouble she could possibly create in two days. Finally he said she could go but warned her against making trouble. She said that this warning was given in a paternal way. Lord Malvern was Doris Lessing's family doctor when she was a child in Salisbury.

4. During her stay on the Copperbelt, she made no secret of the fact that she was a Communist. She appeared surprised at the amount of publicity her visit had received and gave a warning that there would be trouble within ten years with the Africans. Her sympathies clearly lay with the African Congress.

5. On the 11th May, she went to Lusaka and met Harry Nkumbula, Kenneth Kaunda, Martin Fallon of the 'Central African Post', Harry Franklin, M.L.C., and S. H. Chileshe, M.L.C. During her visit to the African National Congress Headquarters in Lusaka she expressed sympathy with the Congress-inspired boycott campaign and said that, so long as there was no violence, boycotts were the only effective way through which Congress could break the colour bar. Mrs Lessing also visited the Inter-Racial Club at Kabulonga. She thanked Harry Franklin for spending a most pleasant afternoon with her and suggested that he should send her a copy of the Moffat Proposals and anything else which he thought she should have. She expressed the

hope that she would meet him in London and gave him her address as 58, Warwick Road, London, S.W. 5; telephone FREmantle 4097.

6. It is learned from a secret source that Mrs Lessing had a number of documents in her possession including letters of introduction to various people from Commander Thomas Fox-Pitt. R.N. Retd. (a retired Provincial Commissioner from Northern Rhodesia) of the Anti-Slavery Society. These introductions were addressed, inter alia, to:

Chief Gomani, Nyasaland.

Mwase Kazungo, Nysaland.

Loya Masonga, Fort Jameson.

7. Mrs Lessing made a vast number of notes on her many interviews and subjects discussed during her tour and there are good grounds for believing that she had made special reference to Congress 'Shadow' Government. She also wrote a rough manuscript of a story called 'The Uneasy Alliance', while she was at the Lusaka hotel. This story will undoubtedly reveal her great sympathy for African advancement and contempt of the colour bar. Mention will probably be also made of the following subjects:

a) The desire of Nyasaland to secede from the Federation.

b) The more militant attitude of Northern Rhodesia Africans as compared with the 'slave mentality' of Southern Rhodesia Africans.

c) European reliance on their dominant place in society not on merits or education but on skin colour.

d) Capital is pouring into the Rhodesias, nothing can stop Central Africa from becoming a modern capitalist state with almost infinite attractions for investors *provided* the Africans co-operate in the programme. The Administration is attempting to create an efficient and stable labour force but the one thing it is not prepared to grant is any kind of political liberty.

8. Mrs Lessing criticises strongly talk of partnership when there is such a very obvious colour bar;
she is believed to have said that the reason why
the Federation is an 'uneasy alliance' is because
the legislation of Southern Rhodesia is closely mod-
elled on that of the Union of South Africa, while
Northern Rhodesia and Nyasaland have been administered
as Protectorates on behalf of the African people by
the Colonial Office.

9. She considers that the danger spot for the
Administration lies in African Trade Unionism in
Northern Rhodesia. The African Mineworkers' Union has
now 43,000 members and the Northern Rhodesia African
National Congress has 80,000 members, in her view.
She thinks that Southern Rhodesia has no intention of
allowing a similar independence of mind to spread to
their country.

10. She also said that she had not met one European
who was enthusiastic about Federation; that all the
Africans whom she met were strongly opposed to it;
that Southern Rhodesia African leaders told her pas-
sionately that their people had to live in conditions which were very much the same as those in South
Africa and that they would support their brothers up
North lest they too should have to live the same way.
Mrs Lessing said that the Northern Rhodesia Africans
seemed extremely sceptical of this 'support' from the
South since they despise the lack of spirit of those
in Southern Rhodesia.

11. Mrs Lessing did however make the point that
the social colour bar is loosening a little, but only
among a European minority. There are, in her view,
a few white people who invite Africans, Indians and
Coloured to their homes but they are regarded with disapproval by the majority. The Inter-Racial Association,
she says, is now considered respectable but somewhat
cranky. She considers that Federation has been bull-
dozed through against the wishes of all the African
inhabitants. Regarding Nyasaland, she says that it
has a strong Congress but is a completely agricultural

country; its role is to provide a reservoir of cheap labour for other countries. She thinks that the only possible weapon in the hands of the Nyasaland Chiefs would be to instruct their people not to allow themselves to be recruited for outside labour, but this, she says, would cut off Nyasas from contact with the modern world.

12. Finally, she makes the point, which must sum up her reconnaissance for International Communism – which was probably the main reason for her visit – that by far the most sensitive part of the whole Federation lies on the Copperbelt with its concentration of labour where the Administration is attempting to curb African aspirations. She says it was invigorating to speak with men, whom she considered able and fearless, who lead Congress and the African Mineworkers' Union. She speaks slightingly of European leaders as 'fatherly gentlemen'. Meeting the dynamic young African leaders is like moving from the nineteenth to the twentieth century. She considers that the latter flatly contradict what the white people intend for Central Africa. There are in her view two different worlds.

18.

PF 97, 471/E.2/KCT
SLO Central Africa
20 June 1956

1. Please refer to your PF 86 of 14 May 1956 enclosing FISB's PFB 187 of 12 May.

2. We have no trace of Wilfred Gordon McDonald Partridge, mentioned by FISB as a possible contact of Mrs Lessing.

3. We shall certainly let you know if we hear that Mrs Lessing is intending to return to Rhodesia permanently.

4. You will appreciate that it might not be possible for us to pass you this information and agree
to the Federal Immigration authorities' declaring Mrs
Lessing a prohibited immigrant *before* she starts her
journey. Such action could very easily prejudice our
source of information.

19.

Temple Bar 2151 (Communist Party H.Q.)
Incoming 10.7.56
Doris Lessing to Idris Cox

Doris said Idris had asked her to come to a meeting –
would Wednesday July 18 be suitable? Idris said it
would: the meeting was at 7.00. Doris did not think
she would be there as soon as that, so Idris said
they would get on with other business and leave hers
till 7.30. Most people would have read her material
in *World News* and *Tribune*, so what they really wanted
was an inside report.

20.

With the compliments of the Security Liaison Officer,
Central Africa.
To: Head Office
PFB 16th July 1956

Mrs Doris May Lessing
Activities in Southern Rhodesia on return from her
visit to Northern Rhodesia on 25th April until her
departure on 17th May 1956.
    Doris Lessing's activities on her return were in
line with those of her visit to Northern Rhodesia and
the previous part of her stay at Salisbury. (Already

reported.) She, and her communist companion Paul Hogarth, whose return from South Africa to Salisbury coincided with Lessing's, were in frequent contact with their communist friends, extremist Africans and others who hold pronounced views on racial questions. Including her first visit, she made well over half a hundred contacts during the time she was in Salisbury: these contacts varied from individual interviews to meetings at the houses of Africans and of one or two Europeans, and a gathering at the house of the representative of the Indian High Commissioner at Salisbury, Nirmaljet Singh.

2. On their return to Salisbury on 25th April, Lessing and Hogarth re-established themselves at the house of Carol Nathan and Dorothy Zelter, 47 Lawson Avenue, Salisbury, and used this as their headquarters.

3. The contacts they made have been noted in detail and where necessary follow-up enquiries have been put in hand. Those of more general interest are mentioned below.

4. Doris Lessing spent the morning of the 29th April at the house of Elias Mtepuka, in the Harare Township, in conference with a number of politically minded Africans. Mtepuka is a free lance journalist who made a study-tour of India in 1954/55. The tour was sponsored by the Indian Government. Mtepuka, on his return, wrote some good objective articles and had obviously acquired mixed feelings regarding India and its people. Others present at Mtepuka's house included Charles Mzingeli, General Secretary of the Reformed Industrial and Commercial Workers Union and vice-chairman of the Inter-racial Association of Southern Rhodesia; J. C. W. Malifa, the energetic leader in Salisbury of the Nyasaland African Congress together with Moses Chimukwapura, a committee member of the Salisbury branch; J. G. S. Chingattie, a politically-minded insurance agent; G. Tembo, who describes himself as the representative in Southern Rhodesia of the Northern Rhodesia African National Congress; Lawrence Vambe, Chief Editor for African

Newspapers Limited; D. K. Chisiza, a Nyasa employed as interpreter and shorthand typist in the Salisbury office of the India High Commissioner (there are some indications that Chisiza holds extreme anti-Federation sentiments); two others in attendance were George Nyandoro and Enock Dumbutshena, both of whom displayed a strongly nationalistic spirit at a recent meeting of the African National Youth League. It is said that Lessing and Harry Chimowitz (of Avondale, Salisbury a civil engineer of Russian/Jewish parents mentioned in our previous report on Lessing), presented Chisiza with a new typewriter so that he can keep Lessing informed of future activities. Chimowitz had conducted Lessing to the meeting. Reports of what transpired are vague: it has been suggested that Lessing was trying to form a 'cell' amongst these African leaders, but the reliability of the source of this suggestion is not known. Certainly, those attending hold strong views on racial matters. Lessing is reported to have told the gathering that Communism will come to the Federation whether or not the government permits it.

5. Lessing and Hogarth the same afternoon, the 29th April, left for Kariba where she took copious notes and he sketched. (Lessing has subsequently published a tendentious article 'The Kariba Project' in The New Statesmen and Nation, dated the 9th June 1956.)

6. On their return from Kariba they went with Zelter to a gathering which lasted for some four hours at the house of Nirmaljet Singh, the representative in Salisbury of the Indian High Commissioner. It appears that some six or seven Europeans, who have connections with or take an interest in race-relation questions, were present, together with Lawrence Vambe, who brought the visiting American negress, Jean Fairfax. Fairfax, who for the past nine years has been working in Europe and America for the 'American Friends Service Committee' was on a holiday tour in the Federation: she is particularly interested in race relations.

Note: There are strong indications that others at the party were: Philip Mason, the Race-Relations research worker employed by the Royal Institute of International Affairs (Director of Race Relations at

Chatham House, London); Fredrick Daniel John Lacey, an inter-racialist who contested the Highlands by-election for the Rhodesia Labour Party in 1953 (Incidentally Lacey entertained Lessing and Zelter to 'sun-downers' on 5th May), Anthony Beck, a naturalised British subject of Czech origin who has been the subject of vague inconclusive reports suggestive of a communist background; Joseph David Chudy, a naturalised British subject born in Poland, who came to Southern Rhodesia in 1938; Bene Mario Augustino Cloro, born in Southern Rhodesia of Italian parents, who has not previously come to notice; and Charles Patrick Jameson Lewis, partner in the firm of Salisbury solicitors, Messrs. Scanlon and Holderness, who is a member of the Inter-racial Association. Lewis visited Zelter's house two or three times whilst Lessing and Hogarth were staying there.

7. Lessing was again in touch with Frederick Gerald Gardener of the Native Education Department, Umtali on the 3rd May and he was at a dinner party given by the Inter-racialist Hardwick Holderness M.P. at Highlands, attended by Lessing and some of her friends on that date.

8. Some of the dinner dates included two with Aubrey (formerly Abram) Urbach, who is a Polish-born naturalised British Subject. Making up the party on one occasion was Zelter and Abraham Zukas who, with Hogarth, accompanied Lessing. It should be mentioned that Abraham Zukas, the brother of the communist Simon Ber Zukas, was staying at Zelter's house. Abraham Zukas is hoping to gain entry to the United Kingdom to read law at the London School of Economics. As regards Urbach, he has been in Southern Rhodesia since 1935 and is part-owner of the Lydiate Tobacco Grading Company. He was mentioned during the last war at the time of the heyday of the Friends of the Soviet Union but has not otherwise attracted attention in a security sense.

9. A reliable report states that Lessing was taken by Nirmaljet Singh, or some other Indian official, to St Faiths Mission, Rusape, where she lunched with a member of the Mission staff, Ralph Gordon Ibbott who

is in touch with a fellow-travelling Pacifist organisation in the United Kingdom which is interested
in Africa. (Ibbott came to St Faiths as Bursar in
May 1952 and has not to date drawn security attention to himself.) Lessing and her escort had tea with
the Agricultural Instructor, Arthur Guy Clutton-Brock
and his wife. (Clutton-Brock has a wide background
of social work, is a strong advocate of adult education for the African and equal partnership between
Europeans and non-Europeans and is the leader at St
Faiths of an inter-racial farm co-operative. He is a
contact of the Reverend Michael Scott (a prohibited
immigrant to the Federation).

10. Independent activities by Lessing and Hogarth,
during the period of this report consisted of a visit
by the former from 7th to 13th May 1956 to Northern
Rhodesia (already covered in our report PFB 187 of the
4th June 1956 issued to those concerned) and a journey
to Bulawayo by the latter. Hogarth was in Bulawayo from
the 4th to the 7th May 1956. He stayed with Francis
Ivor Williams, the communist contact with whom Lessing
had stayed the previous month. Hogarth spent most of
his time sketching at Bulawayo. He did however have
contact, apart from Williams, with some members of
the Inter-Racial Association, notably Jakob (or Jack)
Geras. (Geras was born at Minsk, Russia on 14.11.1912
and is a close associate of Williams and contacted
the deported communist Simon Ber Zukas during a visit
by Geras to London in 1955.) Hogarth also visited the
home of Ronald Ivor Leavis, the Milton schoolmaster and
author of the novel 'A Voice in Every Wind' which has
been banned in Kenya. Although no subversive activity
has been traced to Leavis since he came to Southern
Rhodesia with the RAF in 1941, he has been suspected
of leftist sympathies for some years. Hogarth on his
return to Salisbury proceeded to Northern Rhodesia by
air whilst Doris Lessing was in that territory.

11. A farewell party for Lessing and Hogarth was
given by Zelter on the 16th May 1956. Those present
included persons mentioned previously in reports on

Lessing's activities during her visit, namely Abraham Zukas, Aubrey Urbach, Frederick Karl Baraf, a natural-ised government health inspector and his wife. Others were: Charles Patrick Jameson Lewis and Anthony Beck (see para. 6 above) and some four or five persons with artistic backgrounds but no security traces, and Mrs Zelter's mother, Mrs Dowland.

12. Lessing is reported by a well placed source whilst in the Federation to have expressed the view that Communism is the only answer to African nation-alism and that Northern Rhodesia made a mistake in deporting Simon Ber Zukas, who would have been a sta-bilising influence on the Africans there. In a message published in the issue of the South African communist paper *New Age* dated 31st May 1956, she said she hoped to return to Africa soon. A wish which in the interest of security it would seem undesirable to gratify in view of her various activities during her stay in the Federation.

21.

Section and Officer of origin: F.4/ix
Typing Date: 25.7. 56

Report
African Committee
  1. A meeting of the African Committee was held at King Street on Wednesday, 18 July. Those present were: [names illegible].
  2. The main subject of the meeting was Central African Federation, and Doris Lessing had been in-vited to make a report on her visit there. The report she gave kept very closely to the article in *World News* (attached).
  2. She also spoke of the lack of African under-standing of how best to conduct a fight against such things as (i) the taking away of their land (which she

said was the most burning issue in Northern Rhodesia and Nyasaland, particularly the latter); (ii) the industrial colour bar; (iii) poor living conditions, etc.

3. In Southern Africa there is an African movement run by Charles Mzingeli. He has been leading movements of one kind or another for years. Doris Lessing's opinion is that his current one is no good, and what is worse, is 'cutting the throats of other movements'. However, he is the only leader of any consequence and he must be made use of.

Comments by Consumer Section
This is a very interesting report indeed and we can, to a large extent, confirm the accuracy of Doris Lessing's impressions. [...]

2. I should like, if I may, to have a copy of this report to send to SLO Central Africa who would be extremely interested and might be able to resolve one or two points of detail.

[...]

L. T. Highett

22.

Extract for File No. PF 97, 471
Name: Lessing
Receipt Date: 30.7.56

Ethel May from Kay
Kay told Ethel she had not been able to get any information about people who took children's lectures and at last she had come back to Ethel; she had been to Hymie Fagan, Phil Piratin, Joan Carritt, Jenny Miles. Finally Phil had said that he thought Ethel would have the records. Ethel said Joan Carritt was in charge, she did all the correspondence.

Ethel asked if Kay wanted a list of people [illegible] who were available. She could tell from her memory who took some of the lectures at the first school which was held, Francis Apraraimian took science, Alan Gifford took music and Doris Lessing took writers and the novel. Alan Gifford was West Middlesex, his lecture on music was extremely popular, it was an illustrated thing. Ethel was sorry they had not got his address but West Middlesex should have it. Ethel thought the fourth lecturer was Peter Mather; his address was: 16, Barclay Oval, Woodford Wells, Essex.

23.

Security Liaison Office,
P.O. Box 683
Salisbury,
Southern Rhodesia
27July 1956
To: Head Office

Doris Lessing and Charles Mzingeli
The following report has been received from the CID in Bulawayo:
    'It may interest you to know that Doris Lessing has been appointed to the Central and East African Committee of Fenner Brockway's Movement for Colonial Freedom (which she claims has the support of 110 members at Westminster) and has asked Charles Mzingeli to keep her supplied with any new legislation and newspaper cuttings of events and speeches, etc., which illustrate differential racial treatment. She emphasizes the need for accuracy in matters which are to be brought up in Parliament.'
    For Security Liaison Officer,
    Central Africa
    [signature illegible]

24.

Extract for File No. PF 97, 471
Name: Doris Lessing
Receipt Date: 28.8.56
*Extract from F.I.S.E. Security Intelligence Review,
Rhodesia and Nyasaland, No.10, covering 1st June–15th
August 1956, reference no. SFB 8, forwarded by SLO
Central Africa, mentioning Doris Lessing*

Communist Activity
5. The communist journalist and authoress Doris
Lessing (see Review No. 9 paragraph 6 and 7), who
recently spent seven weeks in the Federation, is reliably reported to have been made a member of the
Central and East African committee of the Movement for
Colonial Freedom, of which Fenner Brockway M.P. is the
chairman. It may be expected that she will endeavour
to exploit racial questions, as she is known to have
sought a source to keep her supplied with news from
the Federation illustrating differences in the treat-
ments of the various races. She has already published
an article on this theme in the British communist
paper *World News*, dated the 7th July 1956: it dealt
with the 'Central African Federation'. The article,
naturally, is pro-African, somewhat scathing and al-
leges that the pattern emerging, with minor differences in the three territories of the Federation, 'is
that of *apartheid*, but apartheid with is claws still
sheathed'.

25.

SLO Central Africa
2 September 1956

    1. Thank you for your reports dealing with Doris
Lessing's recent visit to Central Africa.

2. You may be interested to know that we have now been fortunate enough to obtain from a reliable source an idea of the impressions Doris Lessing formed as a result of her visit. She has told certain leading Communists in this country about the work she did while in Africa and has also given her views on various points as indicated in paragraph 3 onwards:

3. Mrs Lessing is believed to have spoken disparagingly of Charles Mzingeli in Southern Rhodesia, but to have said that, as he is the only leader who is of any calibre, use must be made of him. In Northern Rhodesia and Nyasaland the local Congress movements were fettered by their own nationalism.

4. She appears to think highly of Kaunda in Northern Rhodesia and is known to have praised his organisation. She is critical of its attitude to the Indians though prepared to lay the responsibility for this on the attitude of the membership. She is reported to have spoken well of Nkoloma.

5. Communist influences in the Federation is small according to Mrs Lessing; she claims to know of no Communists in Northern Rhodesia and Nyasaland and only four or five in Southern Rhodesia. The chief of these was Ivor Williams who had done a 'good job' and was facing deportation. Mrs Coleman, with whom Williams worked, was not a Communist but a 'liberal'. Another friend of Williams, Rolek Bango, an acquaintance of Desmond Buckle has been mentioned by Mrs Lessing, as a member of the 'Williams group'.

6. In Salisbury itself there appeared to be no Communists. Mrs Lessing mentioned Harry Chinowitz and Jack Greers of whom she did not hold a high opinion, and in the same way she did not consider Zelter to be a Communist.

7. Our source states also that Mrs Lessing has been recommending that every effort should be made to get into touch with Africans coming from the Federation to the UK. She has also mentioned some Indian trade representatives, whom she describes as 'agitators, but who had been sent out most usefully' by the Indian Government.

8. It is further believed on reliable authority that Mrs Lessing is occupied with the possibility of making use of Cairo radio where, she says, Simon Zukas has a contact; she and Zukas have worked out a number of cover addresses to receive information. An unnamed Zanzibar African has been mentioned by Lessing in connection with this project but source does not state where or who he is. Any help that you can give locally towards uncovering these addresses will be of the greatest value.

9. Mr de Quehen has seen the original of this report.

L. T. Highett

26.

Extract for File No. PF 97, 471
Name: Lessing Doris
Receipt Date: 18.9.56
Extract from petition sent by Jack Lindsay (Communist) with letter to Comrade Gollan, 16 King St., W.C.1. [mentioning]: Lessing.

This Committee meeting of the Writers' Group wishes to express its disapproval of the Executive Committee's resolution on the *The Reasoner* [a communist publication].

We strongly urge the Executive to take no disciplinary action in view of the fact that the fundamental issues involved are to be discussed at the January Conference of the entire Party.

Those present voted as follows:
Against: Nil
Abstained: Kay Thomas
In favour: Doris Lessing

27.

CONFIDENTIAL
From: The Chief Constable
Kingston upon Hull
To: Parliament Street B.O.
London, S.W. 1.
Date: 16th October 1956

Name: Doris Lessing
[...]
I am informed that Doris Lessing will be the speaker
at a public meeting to be held under the auspices
of the Association for African and Asian Affairs at
the Co-operative Hall, Kingston upon Hull on the
27th October 1956. Her subject will be 'Africa in
Ferment'.
    (Copy to: Commander, Special Branch, London, S.W.1.)
    Chief Constable
    [signature illegible]

28.

CONFIDENTIAL
Copy for PF 97, 471, Lessing
12th October 1956

Dear Sir,
The Reasoner
Thank you very much for your letter of 19th September
1956 and for the copy of the second number of *The
Reasoner*.
    Doris Lessing, for whom our reference number is
PF 97,471, is a novelist, who is thought highly of
in Communist circles; she has been known to us as a
member of the Communist Party for some years, having
first come to notice in 1954, when she took a leading

part in the activities of the Salisbury Branch of the Rhodesian Friends of the Soviet Union.

Hyman Levy who is Head of the Department of Mathematics at the Imperial College of Science, London University, is a well known Communist as is also Ronald Meek, who is a lecturer in Political Economy at Glasgow University.

Yours faithfully,

for Director General

[signature illegible]

29.

Extract for File No. PF 97, 471
Name: Lessing
Date of contents: 2.10.56

18.05 Dutt, Cox, Chimen Abramsky and George Hardy holding a meeting, (a Working Committee) and discussing London Council of the MCF.

[...]

They passed on to the question of nomination for the London Council committee (MCF). Cox felt that they could not get very far on this without consulting Kay, but added that there were two people they should bear in mind – Doris Lessing and Montague Slater. The latter, he said, was going to the Gold Coast next month - presumably only temporarily.

WARNING
No action is to be taken on this material without reference to the responsible section, nor may its contents be disclosed outside the Service without permission.

30.

Extract for File No. PF 94, 471
Name: Lessing
Date of contents: 4.10.56

14.00 Cox was dictating [...].

Cox's next epistle was to Doris Lessing, 58, Warwick Road, S.W. 5. and was to be sent on plain paper. He commenced with:

"Dear Doris, I had intended writing you yesterday after reading the news about your elevation to the 'honourable' position of an 'undesirable immigrant'. You have now joined the ranks of several more of our comrades who have received this distinction, and it seems to me that something more needs to be done about this shameful system of keeping all progressive people from Britain from the African territories.

"I had intended writing to you in any case as to whether we could have a talk about the possibility of you being associated with the Movement for Colonial Freedom – possibly you are already a member but I feel that perhaps you could be of greater assistance [and undertake] even greater activity in this field.

"I know you are always extremely busy but what I have in mind would not unduly interfere with your present activity (s?) [*sic*]. Is it possible for you to give me a ring to let me know when it would be convenient for us to have a talk on this matter?

"I am going away to Yorkshire on Saturday and will not be back until Friday of next week, so I'm afraid it will be the end of next week or early the following week."

WARNING
No action is to be taken on this material without reference to the responsible section, nor may its contents be disclosed outside the Service without permission.

31.

Metropolitan Police
Special Branch
17th day of October 1956

With reference to Chief Superintendent's minute on marginally quoted file for a comprehensive report on Doris May Lessing:

She is a fairly well known novelist. She was born on 22nd October 1919 in Persia, her parents being Captain Alfred Cook Taylor, and Emily Maude, formerly McVeagh. In 1939 she married Frank Charles Wisdom; they had one son and one daughter: the marriage was dissolved in 1943. In 1945 she married Gottfried Anton Nicolai Lessing, who was born in Leningrad on 14th December 1914, and was of German nationality; they had one son: this marriage was dissolved in 1949. Her publications include: *The Grass is Singing* in 1950; *This was the Old Chief's Country* in 1951; *Martha Quest* in 1952; *Five* in 1953; and *A Proper Marriage* in 1954. She received the Somerset Maugham award from the Society of Authors in 1954.

This woman occupies the top floor flat at No. 58, Warwick Road, S.W. 5 with her son, now aged about 10 years. No trace of the birth of this child can be found in official records, and it is believed that he was brought to this country by his mother when she first arrived here from Southern Rhodesia in April 1949.

Mrs Lessing first came to notice on 28th June 1952, when she was reported as having left Northolt Airport for Moscow as a member of 'Authors' World Peace Appeal'. On her return to this country, she spoke at a meeting of that group at Friends House, Euston Road, W.C., and contended that the Russian people were thinking and talking only in terms of peace (400/51/ 194). In 1952, she also supported the Kensington Peace Committee; and was a speaker at a meeting of the West London branch of 'Teachers for Peace' held at 15, Ladbroke Grove House, Ladbroke Grove, W. 11, on 1st November 1952 (400/52/43). She last came to notice in connection with 'Peace' activities as a speaker at a conference held under the auspices of 'Authors' World Peace Appeal', at 164 Shaftesbury Avenue, W.1. on 14th March 1954.

On 2nd October 1952, she spoke on her visit to Russia at a meeting of the Society for Cultural Relations with the USSR held at 14, Kensington Square, W. 8. (400/49/2).

On 9th July 1953, she was a signatory on the form of application for the registration of the Peoples Bocks Co-operative Society, Ltd., of 28/29, Southampton Street, Strand, W.C. 2, with the Registrar of Friendly Societies. This society made little progress and her activities on its behalf were very limited (347/53/5). In the same year she was reported as being a member of the Holland Ward (Kensington) Branch of the Communist Party (301/MP/5372E).

On 17th August 1954, she was reported to be a member of the Management Committee of the Russia Today Book club, set up by the British Soviet Friendship Society (400/53/63).

Mrs Lessing was a speaker at the meeting of the 7th Annual Conference of the National Cultural Committee of the Communist Party held at St Pancras Town Hall on 30th January 1955. There she spoke of the sneering attitude of the intellectual press, including the *Times* and the *Manchester Guardian*, towards the working class, and condemned their failure to support the efforts of the working class (400/43/75).

She last came to notice as having sent a letter of support and goodwill to the 4th National Assembly of Women held at St Pancras Town Hall on 8th July 1956 (400/54/125).

I have been reliably informed that Mrs Lessing has used her home as a meeting place for varying numbers of people, many of whom are coloured. These people have been known to use her home during her frequent absences. A suggestion that immoral practices were the reason for the numerous visitors has not been substantiated and it can be safely assumed that these meetings were for the furtherance of the Communist cause. Recently there have only been a small number of callers.

Mrs Lessing is active on behalf of the Communist Party, and it is known that newspapers printed in the Russian language are delivered to her regularly. She contributes articles to the *Daily Worker*, the last one dated 16th October 1956 (copies attached), relates to the lack of political liberties in Central Africa, of which she is a prohibited immigrant.

Doris May Lessing is the holder of British Passport No. 242961, and copies of her photograph, which is a good likeness, are attached. She is known to me and her description is: Age 37 years; height 5' 4"; plump build; brown hair; hazel eyes; tanned complexion.

Constable
[signature illegible]
Superintendent
[signature illegible]
Chief Superintendent
[signature illegible]

32.

Extract for File No. PF 97, 471
Name: Lessing
Receipt Date: 18.10.56
Cutting from Security Intelligence Review - Rhodesia & Nyasaland, [Mentioning], Lessing.

Communist activity.
5. Doris Lessing has continued her activities in England. A tendentious article of hers on the strikes on the Copperbelt is reported to have been published in a Left-wing paper. It is known from secret sources that Doris Lessing has not much of an opinion of African leadership in Southern Rhodesia, thinks more highly of Congress leadership in Northern Rhodesia and feels that communist influence is small in the Federation.

33.

Metropolitan Police
Special Branch
Ref. PF 97, 471
24th October 1956

Since submitting my report on Doris May Lessing (RF
402/50/398; MI5 PF 97, 471), of 18th October 1956.

This woman has come to our notice as the author of
a letter to the second issue of the *The Reasoner* – in
September 1956 – a paper published by John Saville,
152, Westbourne Avenue, Hull, Yorkshire and edited by
Saville and E. P. Thompson, both Communist intellectuals who are in revolt against the leadership of the
Communist Party (347/56/21/).

Her attitude to the present conflict in the Party
is brought out in the following extracts:

The fact that you felt impelled to publish an independent Communist journal seems to me of more significance even than the material you print – which
I find valuable.

Recently I was at a meeting of the party group
where a member of the party administration was present to hear criticisms by comrades of party policy
since the 20th Congress. For some two hours we were
sharply demanding, in various forms, new thinking, a
fresh approach, a return to honest intellectual conflict. The comrade from King Street listened patiently,
and replied in a series of defensive platitudes which
reflected all the attitudes of mind we had been at-
tacking. The point is that this comrade, an intelli-
gent and devoted man, had not the faintest notion what
we were talking about.

One of the most interesting and frightening of the
reactions to the 'revelations' is the attitude of mind
expressed by the phrase 'you intellectuals'. It is a
phrase which inevitably emerges during the course of
a conversation with any of the comrades in leading

positions; and is only yet another of the defensive rationalisations against clear thought.

What we have to demand, I think, is not scape-goats, confessions and breast beatings; but a re-examination of our basic thinking; and this should be done at a full Party Congress devoted not to pious platitudes and affirmations of support for Communism, which should surely be taken for granted by now; but to hard thinking. I am in absolute disagreement with the attitude that open conflict will split the party; on the contrary, I believe that it is only open con-flict resulting in a policy reflecting the various trends in the party which will save it from disintegrating into ineffective little splinter groups. If the atti-tude of mind represented by *The Reasoner* (with which I am in full agreement) can make itself felt at such a congress, then I think its publication will be jus-tified. But you should do everything you can to pre-vent it from becoming something like 'a revolt of the intellectuals'.

The fact is, that [if] we did keep quiet, and if the same situation arose, we would probably keep quiet again. What we have to do is to make it impossible for the same situation to arise. But above all, we must accept our responsibility for having been part of the thing, our responsibility for the good and for the bad.

As long as groups, or individuals, hurl abuse at each other, trying to fasten the blame on each other, it shows we have not begun to accept the implications of what has happened.

We have all been part of the terrible, magnificent, bloody, contradictory process, the establishing of the first Communist regime in the world, which has made possible our present freedom to say what we think and to think again creatively.

Submitted.

Constable

Superintendent

Chief Superintendent

34.

Extract for File No. PF 97, 471
Name: Lessing
Date of contents: 15.10. 56

11.00 Cox was dictating:
   Next letter to Doris Lessing, 58, Warwick Road, saying: When I read your letter, I felt rather humbled at the enormous activity on which you are engaged, and which other comrades not directly involved do not seem to appreciate. I knew that you were associated with the Central African Committee of the NCF, but wasn't aware of all the other strings which you seem to have on your hands. In any case, what I had in mind was the possibility of you attending the London Area Conference of the MCF on November 3rd, and possibly working with the London Area Council. From what you state in your letter it is quite clear that this would be extremely difficult if not impossible. However, if you feel at any time there is some value in consulting with me on some of the problems which arise, I shall be only too glad to make myself available at your convenience.

35.

Extract for File No. PF 97, 471
Name: Lessing Doris
Date of Contents: 18.10.56

17.53 Dutt asked, 'What happened to those things you were going to approach?' and received the reply from Cox that he had written to Doris Lessing (a letter to Lessing quoted in K.S. 27 of 4.10.56 at approximately 14.00) and it seemed that he had had a 'most pathetic letter' back from her about her present commitments including commitments with MCF – she's on the East Africa National Committee of the MCF, Central Africa.

She's now engaged on a campaign about this declar-
ation of her being a ... [sic] of the Labour Monthly
letters. She ends the letter up with underlining
etc., 'please no more committees'. Cox said that he'd
not press the matter any further and merely replied
to her letter in 'friendly terms'.

36.

Extract for File No. PF 97, 471
Name: Lessing Doris
Date of contents: 23.10.56

13.39 then he dictated a letter to Doris Lessing, 58,
Warwick Road, S.W. 5.:
Dear Doris,
   There is one matter which has cropped up in which
you might be interested, both from the political and
financial angle. I am not able to explain it by letter,
but if it would be convenient for you to call in one
day, I can explain the proposal to you. Let me make
it clear that this has nothing to do with the subject matter of the previous letter, but it is in fact
a proposal to become the London correspondent of a
progressive journal in another country which will be
both of political value and also give a small financial return for your trouble.
   If you feel that it is not possible for you to
consider the proposal, then the absence of any reply
will make this clear to me. If, however, you feel
interested, just give me a ring on the phone to let me
know when you are passing my way and we can .... [sic].
   Best wishes, yours fraternally ...
   13.46 Cox finished dictating.

Parting with the Communist Party and the Waning of Security Interest

1956 (2)

In November 1956 Soviet tanks invaded Hungary to quell an uprising there. This brutal action prompted many left-wing intellectuals to question their loyalties to Soviet communism.

37.

```
Extract for File No. PF 97, 471
Name: Lessing
Receipt Date: 20.11.56
```
Copy of Telecheck on Temple Bar 2151, Communist Party H.Q.; conversation between John Campbell and George Mathews, mentioning Lessing.

```
Incoming. 20.11.56. DAILY WORKER LINE.
John Campbell asked for John Gollan but he was in a
meeting. Campbell thought Gollan would be interested
in what he had to say and they got George Mathews
out of the same meeting. He read out a letter he had
received:
```

> All of us have for many years advocated Marxist ideas,
> both in our own special fields and in political discus-
> sion in the Labour Movement. We feel therefore that we
> have a responsibility to express our views as Marxists
> in the present crisis of international Socialism.
>
> We feel that the uncritical support given by the Executive
> Committee of the Communist Party to Soviet action in

Hungary is the undesirable culmination of years of dis-
tortion of facts, a period where British comrades have
to think out (??????????) [*sic*] political problems for
themselves. We had hoped that the revelations made at
the 20th Congress of the CPSU would have made our leadership and press realise that Marxist ideas will only be
acceptable to the British Labour Movement if they arise
from the truth about the world we live in.

The exposure of the grave crimes and abuses in the USSR
and the recent revolt of workers and intellectuals
against the pseudo Communist bureaucracies and police
systems of Poland and Hungary have shown that for the
past twelve years we have made a political analysis on
a false presentation of the facts. Not on a note of ...
[*sic*], for we still consider the Marxist method to be
correct. If the Left Wing and Marxist trend in the Labour
Movement is to win support, ... [*sic*] Party must be utterly
repudiated. This includes the immediate repudiation of
the latest outcome of this evil past, the E.C.'s under-
writing of the current errors of Soviet Policy.

Not all the signatories agreed with everything in this
letter, but all are in sufficient sympathy with its general intention to sign with this reservation.

Signed:

Chimen Abramsky, Henry Collins, R. H. Hilton, E. G.
Hobsbawm, George Houston, Hyman Levy, Ronald (?) Meek,
Robert Browning, Benjamin Farrington, Christopher Hill,
Paul Hogarth, Doris Lessing, Jack Lindsay E. A. Thompson.

George said he understood E. A. Thompson, the
Nottingham professor, had left already. Campbell said
he evidently had not. George supposed Campbell wanted
to know what to do, and he would ring him back. Unable
to hear this properly. Campbell speaks indistinctly.
It might be something more like, 'this mask of the
achievements'.

38.

Section and Officer of origin: F.4/MK
Report
Typing Date: 28.12. 56

Doris Lessing has resigned from the British Communist Party.

1957

I.

Section and Officer of origin: D.1/JRF
Report
Typing Date: 9.1.57

Doris Lessing
[...]
   3. Doris Lessing informed Source that she thought the British Communist Party was hopeless and gutless over Hungary and appeared to be without any future. For that reason she left.
   4. Source feels that Doris Lessing is a Marxist at present in search of a Communist Party she can support. Source thinks she is fed up with the Russians for not paying her £1,000 they owe her for the translation of her novels. Source describes her as an attractive, forceful, dangerous woman, ruthless if need be, even wavering in a forceful way and not prepared to do anything against any form of Communism.

2.

PF 97, 471
18th January 1957

Dear General Rademeyer,
Doris May Lessing.
   1. You will be interested to learn that Doris
Lessing has resigned from the British Communist Party.
She is believed to have disagreed with the Party executive on the line taken by the Party towards events
in Hungary.
   2. Despite her resignation, we have no reason to
believe that Mrs Lessing's fundamental Marxist con-
victions have in any way changed.
   3. *Central Africa only (not on original).*
You may regard this copy as an action copy and pass
the information to your links if you so desire.
   Yours sincerely,
   A. S. Martin
   for Director General

Major General C. I. Rademeyer,
Commissioner for South African Police,
P.O. Box No: 1895
Pretoria

3.

Extract for File No. PF 97,471
Name: Lessing
Date of contents: 13.11.57

11.16 Cox was dictating some letters.
   First was to Doris (surname not available), 58,
Warwick Road, Earls Court, S.W. 5. This began 'Dear
Doris' and went on to say that Cox had been intending
for some time to contact her. He apologised for rushing

away from 'Focus' in September without having a chat
and saying 'Good bye', but the opportunity did not
occur. Cox said that the most important reason for
writing was the present situation in Central Africa and
the 'frightening prospect' that the proposed Bill of
the Federal Assembly would be accepted in both Houses
of the British Parliament, despite the objections of
the African Affairs Board. He was doing all he could
do get the appropriate organisations to take action
in this matter and he understood that pressure would
be exercised to get a debate in the Commons before
the 40 days grace expires on 10th December. Though he
realised that Doris was anxious to devote all her time
available to get on with her 'valuable work', he felt
that her personal association with Rhodesia and her
knowledge of the situation would bring even greater
pressure to bear in the right quarters. He thought it
might be useful if she could spare an hour to have an
exchange of views on what she felt could and should be
done in this matter. He suggested coming along to her
place or meeting her at some other convenient place
and would fit in with any time suitable to her. He
added that he was writing to one or two other friends
on this matter and hoped to get things moving a little
faster on the right lines. Cox told Rose to enclose a
stamped envelope but with no address on it.

17.26 Cox went on to say that he had had a long
talk with Doris Lessing, who he met down at Dorothy's
place in Oakhurst a couple of months ago. This had
been quite a friendly talk. He had also written to
her saying it would be useful to have a chat. Pillay
thought Doris was 'all right', although she had left
the Party and made a few other remarks about her. She
had told Cox quite frankly that she wanted to get on
with her work and did not want to accept political
responsibility for giving an answer on problems which
she felt were not in her line. That was basically her
attitude. However, the chats had been quite friendly
at Oakhurst and Cox had hoped to have a final one to
speak about her position in the Party. He thought she

would ultimately find her way back, and anyway did not
regard her as anti-Party. Pillay agreed saying that
she did not take any anti-Party attitudes.

1958

I.

Extract for File No. PF 97, 471
Name: Lessing
Dated: 24.1.58
Original from: Summary of World Broadcasts
Extracted on: 18.2.58

Doris Lessing's Books Recommended
In a literary broadcast for youth in the home service,
listeners were advised to increase their knowledge
of Southern Rhodesia by reading the books written by
Doris Lessing, described as a British author who had
come to Africa as a small girl and lived there for
25 years. Her book *This Was the Old Chief's Country*
told about her childhood and about racial discrimination. 'Doris Lessing has not written any books
telling how the little girl grew up and how her consciousness was further formed and consolidated. We
meet her again after she has become already a mature
author, and we know that the alarm and stupefaction
of the little girl have grown to become a sharp conscious protest of the author against the colonial
yoke and racial discrimination.' The young listeners
were advised to read a short story by Doris Lessing
'The Anthill' which exposed the evils of racial discrimination and [recorded] the wonderful friendship
which had sprung up between a white boy and a coloured lad, illegitimate son of a rich British gold
mine owner. (Moscow 08.40. 181.58)

2.

Reference: PF 97, 471
24.2.58

Mrs Lessing's name was entered in the British Suspect
Index on 21 September 1957 when according to the
Circular BS 10127, she was a communist 'who is likely
to visit Africa in the near future'. I suggest that
she no longer qualifies for the Index and her name
shculd be removed.
   F. G. Johnstone
   Cdr. R.N. (Retd)

After 1958

Although Doris Lessing's name was now removed from the British
Suspect Index, it did not mean that the security services had lost interest
in her. They still kept a close eye on her movements and activities.

1.

'Loose minute'
Ref. PF 97, 471
Dated: 29.6.59

Doris Lessing: I refer to your report 34855 dated 15
June on Dorothy Diamond. I should be interested in
further reports on Lessing with particular reference
to her projected visit to the Far East.
   J. E. Day

2.

Extract for File No. PF 97, 471
Date: 24.9.59
*Copy of F4/RMS Source Report re the East German
Cultural Exhibition and extract from the attached
list, mentioning: Lessing.*

Attached is a copy of a list of 'sympathetic' people
in the Cultural field in this country, sent to Mr
Mattey of the East German Cultural Exhibition, who
would be interested to attend a party given by the
exhibitors. The list was mainly compiled by Mrs Moody
of the Screen Viewers' Panel.
Doris Lessing, 58, Warwick Road, S.W. 5

3.

Extract for File No. PF 97,471,
Dated: 25.9.59
*Report regarding the Entertainments Arts Socialist
Association   (Communist   dominated   organisation)
mentioning Lessing*

Attached is a list of the membership of EASA as at
June 1959. [...]; Doris Lessing, 58, Warwick Road,
London, S.W. 5.

4.

Extract from File No. PF 97, 471
Dated: 31.3.60
*Referring to the arrival of Yuri Leonov to take up a
position with the Soviet Trade Delegation*

1. held a cocktail party at his home. Some 28 guests were there, including an American publisher, an American agent (wife of Hugh Greene of the BBC), an American author and his wife, a number of writers including Doris Lessing, the Minister Counsellor of the French Embassy (Wapler), Mr and Mrs Yuri Leonov, of International Book at the STD, and Mrs Marton, a publisher's reader.

2. Leonov was immensely popular, entertaining, eager to talk and to listen. He had a long talk with the American publisher, M. Wapler, Mrs Marston, a serving officer in the British Army, the son of an Irish peer, and Doris Lessing, who agreed to sign a copy of her book for him.

5.

A report on The Committee of 100 (1960: Organisation advocating civil disobedience against Nuclear War) Dated: 26.10.60

On Saturday, 22.10.60, the Committee of 100 held an inaugural discussion meeting of about fifty persons at Friends' House, Euston Road, N.W. 1, from 2 p.m. to 5 p.m. The meeting was private and only those with letters of invitation were admitted. The following are known to have been present: [...] Doris Lessing.

* * * * *

Similar information was recorded on 26.11.62 – that Doris Lessing was one of several writers supporting the Campaign for Nuclear Disarmament. This is the last report on her in the files available to us. Whether Doris was still under surveillance in later years, we do not know. There is no doubt that, all along, she was well aware that she was being kept under observation by the security service. But she was fearless. She was dedicated to the work she was deeply involved in, and did not care if her movements were watched or not. The only thing that she seems not to have known is who was spying on her within her immediate circle. The 'reliable source' on whom the security service largely depended for their information on Lessing must have been amongst those who were close to her; and if she had ever identified this source, it would certainly have caused her much pain. Otherwise Doris Lessing took no notice of the security service – or rather pitied them. In her *modus vivendi*, she seems to have kept to Dr Johnson's recommendation: *ut et mihi vivam et amicis* ('that I may live for my own good and that of my friends').

Epilogue

Doris Lessing as Writer

In 2007, the Nobel Committee justified the award of the Nobel Prize to Doris Lessing, describing her as 'that epicist of the female experience, who with scepticism, fire and visionary power has subjected a divided civilisation to scrutiny'. It is true that Doris displayed fire, and she was certainly a visionary. But to single her out as an 'epicist of the female experience' seems exaggerated, as is the emphasis on the 'divided civilisation' she scrutinized. Examination of the female experience has long been of interest to writers, although perhaps differently handled. And consideration of our civilization, as opposed to barbarism, has occupied thinkers from the very beginning of its existence. Both are issues that have been treated by distinguished writers in times gone by.

When Doris Lessing published her first novel, *The Grass is Singing*, in 1950 she established herself indisputably as a mistress of English prose. The title of the book was borrowed from *The Waste Land* by T. S. Eliot:

> In this decayed hole among the mountains
> In the faint moonlight, the grass is singing
> Over the tumbled graves, about the chapel
> There is the empty chapel, only the wind's home.
> [...]

Doris quotes this verse at the beginning of her book. She also offers another quotation (from an unknown author): 'It is by the failures and misfits of a civilisation that one can best judge its weaknesses.' These epigraphs make us responsive to the spirit in which *The Grass is Singing* was composed.

The style of the language is highly lyrical:

> It was such a lovely, lovely day, with its gusts of perfumed wind, and its gay. glittering sunshine. Even the sky looked different, seen from between the well-known buildings, that seemed so fresh and clean with their white walls and red roofs. It was not the implacable blue dome that arched over the farm, enclosed it in a cycle of unalterable

seasons; it was a soft flower-blue, and she felt, in her exaltation, that she could run off the pavement into the blue substance and float there, at ease and peaceful at last.[1]

The mastery of narrative and situation is also remarkable. *The Grass is Singing* tells us what society was like in Southern Rhodesia in the 1940s. It was dismal. The colonials, most of them English, had come to settle. Many of them arrived after the First World War, wanting simply to own land and to make money. The native Africans served as cheap labour, and were treated like scum: 'A white person may look at a native, who is no better than a dog.'[2] The 'nigger' boys were forbidden to learn English. Most white people thought that it was 'cheek' if a native spoke English: 'Don't talk that gibberish to me,' Mary Turner snapped at the boy.[3] She 'hated their half-naked, thick-muscled black bodies stooping in the mindless rhythm of their work. She hated their sullenness, their averted eyes when they spoke to her, their veiled insolence; and she hated more than anything, with a violent physical repulsion, the heavy smell that came from them, a hot, sour animal smell.'[4] Yet it was to this 'sour animal' that Mary made love sometime later. How was it that she drifted so low? Had she gone mad (as it was assumed), or how desperate was her married life? And did she find solace in 'the superior potency of the native'? That white women should be 'lusting after black penises' seems to have been 'one of the myths furnishing the colonial mind'. But Lessing's own experience destroys this myth. She writes:

> A certain exiled black writer was putting in his time in London. He pursued me for months, full of ardour; he loved me, he could not sleep for thinking of me. Sighs and suffering, the language of romantic despair – the lot. Now, I had never been to bed with a black man. This was because I did not really fancy them. You could say that it was my early conditioning, if it were not that the same conditioning has produced people, but I think mostly men, who yearn for black flesh. It was because of pity for his state that I eventually gave in, expecting to assuage a painful passion. *The actual*

---

1   Doris Lessing, *The Grass is Singing* (London: Michael Joseph, ninth impression, July 1979), 122.
2   *Ibid.*, 176.
3   *Ibid.*, 146.
4   *Ibid.*, 141–2.

sexual contact lasted perhaps three minutes, and then he fell asleep. His snores were such as I had never heard before nor have since.[5]

The Grass is Singing recounts the plight of the white farmers. Very few of them made a fortune. Dick Turner lived in a shabby house. When Mary married him she thought she might buy new furniture, brighten the sordid walls and repair the ceiling – but all in vain. Frustration took hold of her heart and mind. Dick spent all his day in the field, coming back, tired, morose and sullen, with very little to say when at home. Mary had little to do: she 'sat all day, sewing and stitching, hour after hour, as if fine embroidery would save her life.' It failed to do so. She tried to read the books she had collected over the years. They were books she had read with pleasure before; but 'now she turned them over listlessly, she wondered why they had lost their flavour. Her mind wandered as she determinedly turned the pages; and she realized, after she had been reading for perhaps an hour, that she had not taken in a word. She threw the book aside and tried another, but with the same result.'[6] In contrast to Dick Turner's way of life, there was that of Charlie Slatter, 'a proper cockney' to the core 'even after twenty years in Africa'. Slatter had come 'with one idea: to make money. He made it. He made plenty.' He was 'crude, brutal, ruthless'. These two modes of living characterized life in Southern Rhodesia at the time when Doris Lessing left that country.

She arrived in London 'as a bemused colonial',[7] a well-known literary critic has observed. Not only bemused, we must add, but shocked and bewildered. England in 1949, she remembered later, was 'at its dingiest, my personal fortunes at their lowest, and my morale at zero. I also had a small child.'[8] She lived in a 'household crammed to the roof with people who worked with their hands'.[9] And yet, she recalls, 'I can't remember a time

5 Lessing, *Walking in the Shade*, 343.
6 Lessing, *The Grass is Singing*, 75.
7 Peter Conrad, *The Everyman History of English Literature* (London: J. M. Dent, 1985), 701.
8 Doris Lessing, *In Pursuit of the English: A Documentary* (London: Granada Publishing, 1977), 17.
9 *Ibid.*, 13.

when I didn't want to come to England. This was because, to use the word in an entirely different sense, I was English. In the colonies or dominions people are English when they are sorry they ever emigrated in the first place; when they are glad they emigrated but consider their roots are in England; when they are thoroughly assimilated into the local scene and would hate ever to set foot in England again; and even when they are born colonial but have an English grandparent.'[10] Doris considered herself to be English. But she found herself in an unfortunate situation: she did not succeed 'in getting to know an Englishman'. That was 'not because, as the canard goes, Englishmen are hard to know, but because they are hard to meet'.[11]

Doris spent weeks looking for digs to live in, some place that would take a small child, but no English family would accept her. Then 'a household of Italians welcomed the child and me, and my main problem was solved'. Also *The Grass is Singing* brought her an advance, though this was 'at once swallowed up by rent and fees for the nursery school'. She began writing short stories which sold rather well. Then she 'returned abruptly to international politics, communists, the comrades, passionate polemic, and the rebuilding of Britain to some kind of invisible blueprint which everyone shared'.[12] Doris became popular with the communist group: she was accepted as one of them, because of her criticism of white rule in Africa. She was soon taking an active part, performing her 'revolutionary duty in various ways'. She organized petitions in the hope of sparing the Rosenbergs from death in the electric chair; she distributed communist literature; she sold the *Daily Worker* and called at doors in big blocks of flats canvassing for council elections; she organized help for American colleagues in Britain escaping the McCarthy witchhunt. In addition, she visited communist-sponsored peace conferences, and attended a World Conference of Intellectuals initiated by the Soviet Union. She joined not only the Communist Party Writers' Group, but also the British Communist Party itself. And yet she loathed 'the dishonesty and double-dealing characteristic of the comrades'. She especially hated the 'labels': 'Unhappy with

10   *Ibid.*, 14.
11   *Ibid.*, 9.
12   Lessing, *Walking in the Shade*, 19.

communism, I was unhappiest with its language [...].'[13] One day, Doris was invited to a reception hosted by the Soviet Embassy in London, where, she was told, she was to be introduced to a 'very important visitor from Moscow'. Two men in military uniform escorted her. 'They took me,' she records, 'one on each side, to stand in front of a general – I've forgotten his name. Around him were aides I thought of as military staff, but of course they were KGB. He was a squarish, solid man, with eyes like ice, and he was talking entirely in communist jargon: The working class ... fascist imperialists ... peace fronts ... exploited masses ... advancing the cause of communism. I wasn't really listening. What was wrong with me? Was I going to faint? I was cold, and my palms sweated. There was the queerest sensation at the back of my neck – the short hairs there were standing up. I was scared. I was terrified. He was frightening me to death. This has never happened to me since. I think this was where I came closest – touch close – to the murderous horrors of the Soviet Union.'[14]

She did not agree with the Communist Party line on literature, so she left the Party. She now devoted her energies to writing the volumes *Children of Violence*. These are a study in race, gender and age relations, the action entirely confined within the sphere of white colonials in Southern Rhodesia. The life of the native Africans hardly appears in the narrative at all, but the problem of gender identity is described very richly. The chief figure is named Martha Quest. When Doris's autobiographical volumes appeared, it became safe to assume that the story of Martha Quest is actually the story of Doris Lessing when she was in Africa.

Martha Quest is the teenage daughter of English parents. She has her own views on how she should live her life. In particular, her attitude towards the natives is different from that of her mother. When Mrs Quest warns her that she should not walk home alone from the Dumfries Hills because something might happen to her if she 'encountered an evil native' – this wasn't England – Martha laughs 'angrily'. 'Oh, don't be ridiculous,' said Martha. 'If a native raped me, then he'd be hung and I'd be a national heroine, so he wouldn't do it, even if he wanted to, and why should he?'[15]

---

13   *Ibid.*, 36.
14   *Ibid.*, 104–5.
15   Doris Lessing, *Martha Quest* (London: Hart-Davis, MacGibbon, 1952), 54.

When Martha introduces her fiancé to her parents, telling them they are soon to marry, Mrs Quest still hopes that she will remain a virgin, and that her daughter will keep to the English puritan tradition. Martha has, in fact, lost her virginity a long time ago. And when her mother enquires if the pair want to be married at the district church, Martha says 'hotly that they were both atheists, and it would be nothing but hypocrisy to be married in church'.[16] Mrs Quest falls into a rage and writes a ten-page letter to Martha 'in which the phrases *you young people, the younger generation, free-thinkers, Fabian sentimentalists* and words like *immoral*, were repeated in every sentence'.[17] Martha tears the pages up and throws them in the dustbin.

Martha had lost her virginity when she was seduced not by an English colonial, but by a 'Jew-boy'.[18] It was regarded as a profanation to have slept with one of the 'Jew-boys who change their names': 'He's loathsome. Adolph King – trying to pretend he's not a Jew'. Stella, Martha's friend, herself Jewish (though married to a Scotsman) feels disgusted, and disapproves of the affair. Why? – Because what would people say 'about an innocent English girl' being seduced by a 'Jew-boy?' Poor Adolph, suffering a persecution complex, says to Martha: 'Well, they've warned you not to be seen in public with a disgusting Jew.' 'You seem to forget Stella's Jewish herself,' retorts Martha. 'Yes,' replies Adolph, 'but she's from an old English family, she's not scum from Eastern Europe, like me.'[19]

Slowly but sadly, Martha becomes conscious of the fact that she is falling into disgrace. Once when she says she thinks that the natives are 'shockingly underpaid', her fiancé Donovan remarks: 'If you're not careful, Matty dear, you'll become a proper little nigger-lover.' On another occasion, he says: 'Well, Matty, we don't seem to go together at all, do we? I'm simply not broadminded enough for your Jews and your niggers.'[20]

This is perhaps the first time that we learn that a 'Jew-boy' was no better than a 'nigger-boy' in white colonial society. Doris Lessing draws our attention to the fact so that we have to take it in. Previously this contemptible

16   *Ibid.*, 281.
17   *Ibid.*, 275.
18   *Ibid.*, 208–9.
19   *Ibid.*, 220–1.
20   *Ibid.*, 251.

characterization of a people was known to us only in Joseph Goebbels's propaganda hit *Jud-Süss*. Surprisingly those who have written on Doris Lessing do not refer at all to this aspect of life in Rhodesia.

In *A Ripple from the Storm*, Martha Quest is now less interested in sex life. She has become a communist intellectual, an active Stalinist. She is suspicious of Trotskyists, her group believing: that they should be watched; that they should not be allowed to gain control of anything; that they should not be allowed to know that the Soviet-sponsored group existed; that they should be *exposed* at public meetings when they made statements detrimental to the honour of the Soviet Union. As for other people outside the group, they were all deviationists, social democrats, left-wing sectarians, right-wing temporisers.' These terms, the author notes, 'were flung at random and without further definition'.[21] *A Ripple from the Storm* is a study in what it means to be engaged in a group. It helped 'to put that frenetic time when *everyone* was a communist into perspective', Doris wrote later, but it was 'described by many of the comrades as seditious, fouling the nest'. As a work detailing the 'vagaries and dynamics of group behaviour', it explored the mechanisms and dynamics involved in joining and belonging. People join groups, such as a feminist associations, black activist groups, Greenpeace or Animal Rights. They are first attracted to 'the intrigue and excitement'; then they are disillusioned and leave.

> A group is a group is a group – just as a mob is a mob. The machineries that activate them are the same, whatever the cause. If you've been in one, you've been in them all. It is amazing to me that now, when so much is known about the mechanisms and dynamics of group behaviour, there is no attempt, when one is being set up, to make use of this information about what is bound to happen. If there was ever a block in the mind – a barrier, a division – it is this one: 'We do not want to know' about our behaviour.[22]

That was exactly how the Stalinist mind had been managed.

> The Bolsheviks agreed together that they would not be like the revolutionaries of the French Revolution: their own revolution would not devour its children, they

---

21 Doris Lessing, *A Ripple from the Storm* (London: MacGibbon, 1965), 45.
22 Lessing, *Walking in the Shade*, 228–9.

would not kill each other. This noble aspiration, as we know, came to nothing, and they all murdered each other with rhetorical enthusiasm.[23]

And this Martha Quest failed to understand.

A Proper Marriage[24] is anything but 'proper'; it is, rather, an ill-assorted marriage. Martha gets married, and joins a committee to investigate the conditions of the native coloured people. Her marriage is a failure. Her husband spends night after night in the local club, where he is 'made reckless with alcohol'.[25] He is unfaithful to her, and is surprised that his wife sets 'no bounds to his freedom'.[26] Martha is now pregnant. She would like to have an abortion, but then decides against it. Mrs Quest, her mother, is quite happy: 'It'll calm her down.' She hopes it will be a boy, and dreams of sending him to Sandhurst. Martha is hardly able to keep her mind steady. Her husband is seldom at home. It is 'all intolerable'. She finds herself shut up 'in this flimsy little flat, by the rain, because of the baby in the stomach', and forced to agree that her husband can go out with the boys. She is no more than 'the wife of one of the lads. That was all.'[27] She decides to leave her husband and set about living differently. So she becomes an active member of 'The Help for Our Allies Committee' (which means help for the Soviet Union) and a 'Contemporary Politics Discussion Circle' (which obliges her to propagate communist literature). Living differently also means making love to comrades. Moreover, she seeks intimate admirers elsewhere too: during the war, English pilots are being trained in Rhodesia (the local men now being entirely ignored) and there is no common principle governing who one can make love with. This episode is symptomatic. Martha's friend, Maisie, derives enormous pleasure from her liaison with an English airman:

> You know, Matty, I like these English boys, don't you? It'll be awfully hard to go back to our own after knowing them. They treat us quite differently, don't they?

23   *Ibid.*, 229.
24   Doris Lessing, *A Proper Marriage* (London: Granada Pubishing Limited, 1954; this edition: Hart-Davis, MacGibbon, 1964).
25   *Ibid.*, 397.
26   *Ibid.*, 396–7.
27   *Ibid.*, 456.

[…] I never get any sleep. They read more books. They talk about things. They've got culture, that's what it is.[28]

There seems to be no contradiction between a promiscuous life and working towards communist aims. Martha discovers 'rather to her surprise, that she must be an intellectual', but is led to ponder how intellectuals are 'doomed to futility because they always thought about things instead of doing them'. For herself, she must forget her personal anxieties and devote her energy to communism, because 'there might be a revolutionary situation at any moment', and this made 'wasting time on personal matters'[29] seem selfish and trivial.

Martha's responsibilities now include 'stacking pamphlets and books on the Soviet Union into a suit case' for the meetings of Sympathisers of Russia, Help for Our Allies and the Progressive Club. She spends 'one afternoon a week selling *The Watchdog* from house to house in the coloured area'.[30] Her mentor is comrade Anton, a German Jew, head of the communist cell in Rhodesia. He lectures on what a true communist must be:

> A communist, comrades, is a person who is utterly, totally, dedicated to the cause of freeing humanity. A communist must consider himself a dead man on leave. A communist is hated, despised, feared and hunted by the capitalists of the world. A communist must be prepared to give up everything: his family, his wife, his children at a word from the Party. […] A communist must remember that if he has personal weaknesses, it will be laid to the door of the Party. A communist must always order his private life in such a way that the Party cannot be blamed for it. […][31]

With words like these, Anton so brainwashes comrade Martha that she succumbs to his seduction, gets herself divorced and marries him. When they make love, the 'act of sex was short and violent, so short she was uninvolved'.[32] Anton talks about 'his experiences in the revolutionary movement in Germany'. And, as a true communist, he has in the meantime

28 *Ibid.*, 510.
29 *Ibid.*, 692.
30 Lessing, *A Ripple from the Storm*, 9, 13, 31 and 97.
31 *Ibid.*, 39.
32 *Ibid.*, 181.

engaged a redhaired girl to be his mistress. Matty is a good comrade doing good party work and is not a jealous wife. Besides she has a lover of her own, a married Polish Jew. But she becomes fed up with it all. The comrades have not been able to found a single African cell. How could they? Their time is consumed in jumping from one bed to another, in drunken bouts, in indulgence in boastful talk, and in distributing communist propaganda among natives who can barely read. The cause of freeing humanity in Africa never had a start.

Martha now has one single aim: to 'cut Anton out of her consciousness',[33] divorce him and escape to England. Anton himself wants to get away to communist East Germany – but also via Britain. Through his marriage to Martha, he has become a British citizen, and he asks Martha not to file for divorce till they are safely in English territory. Martha agrees. After reaching Britain, Anton writes to his East German comrades telling them about his intention to join the regime. However, as the book recounts: 'the communist government in East Germany did not reply to his letters, to his demands to come home.'[34] It therefore takes a considerable time before Anton gets permission to cross over to East Germany.

Martha's narrative exactly reflects the image of Doris Lessing in her memoirs. Doris tells how, when both she and Gottfried Lessing arrived in London in 1949, Gottfried told her that he had 'formally applied to the East German government to be allowed to return as a citizen. Nothing happened. He applied again. Silence.'[35] Finally the East German government let him in and he got a job in the *Kulturbund*.

The Golden Notebook[36] is not strictly a novel; it is, as the title suggests, a collection of notebooks, a diary, a discourse on various topics, a dialogue with various people conducted by the fictional writer Anna Wulf, who keeps four notebooks and then tries to make sense of all the experiences and impressions within them, many of them mirroring Doris Lessing's own. There are long chapters that can be classified as fiction; there are even passages

33   Doris Lessing, *Landlocked* (London: Granada Pubishing Limited, 1965; this edition: Hart-Davis, MacGibbon, 1965), 131.
34   *Ibid.*, 242.
35   Lessing, *Under My Skin*, 412.
36   Doris Lessing, *The Golden Notebook* (New York: Simon and Schuster, 1962).

one might describe as pornographic, as here in the yellow notebook, when Anna describes her experiences through the novelistic character of 'Ella':

> When Ella first made love with Paul, during the first few months, what set the seal on the fact she loved him, and made it possible for her to use the word, was that she immediately experienced orgasm. Vaginal orgasm that is. And she could not have experienced it if she had not loved him. It is the orgasm that is created by the man's need for a woman, and his confidence in that need.
>
> As time went on, he began to use mechanical means. (I look at the word mechanical – a man wouldn't use it.) Paul began to rely on manipulating her externally, on giving Ella clitoral orgasms. Very exciting. Yet there was always a part of her that resented it. Because she felt that the fact he wanted to, was an expression of his instinctive desire not to commit himself to her. [Paul was afraid of the emotion.] A vaginal orgasm is emotion and nothing else, felt as emotion and expressed in sensations that are indistinguishable from emotion. [...][37]

This sounds as if it were a treatise on sexual indulgence. But Doris does not tell us if harmony in relations between men and women would improve if the issue of doubtful orgasms were settled.

The Golden Notebook has four major sections, with subtitles, 'Free Women'. This evoked a strong response from the feminists, many of them claiming that Doris, a distinguished writer, was enhancing their cause. This claim was partly true. Doris did refer to 'breakdown' or 'crack up' in human relations, especially in marriages, and she supported the Women's Liberation movement, 'because women are second-class citizens'. But this book 'was not a trumpet for Women's Liberation. It described many female emotions of aggression, hostility, resentment. It put them into print. Apparently what many women were thinking, feeling, experiencing, came as a great surprise. Instantly a lot of very ancient weapons were unleashed, the main ones, as usual, being on the theme of *She is unfeminine, She is a man-hater*.'[38] Doris Lessing writes about the frailties of humanity – people's feelings, their temptations, the relation of cause and effect. But she prescribes no recipe. She thought that she 'had written a tract about the sex war, and fast discovered that nothing I said then could change that diagnosis. Yet the essence of the

37   *Ibid.*, 186.
38   *Ibid.*, xii.

book, the organization of it, everything in it, says implicitly and explicitly, that 'we must not divide things off, must not compartmentalise'.[39]

The narrative is not separated by partitions. Rather, we are presented with a literary miscellany. Here, on one page, we have a debate on Marxism, discussion of the revolt in Hungary, and an airing of problems within the Communist Party; then, on the following page, comes a column about an American who is neurotic and ostensibly writing a masterpiece:

> He left his wife. Because she was neurotic. Got himself a girl. Very nice one. Decided she was neurotic. Went back to his wife. Decided she was neurotic. Left her. Has got himself another girl who so far hasn't become neurotic.[40]

In another episode, Ella meets an American businessman. She goes to bed with him [...], but 'she did not come. [...] she understood suddenly that she would never come with this man. She thought: for women like me, integrity isn't chastity, it isn't fidelity, it isn't any of the old words. Integrity is the orgasm. That is something I haven't any control over.'[41] Does this paragraph make any sense? Ella goes on to ask the American about his attitude toward McCarthyism.

> *He:* 'We can't have the Reds taking over.'
> *She:* 'The woman I share a house with is a communist'.[42]

Section 4 in 'Free Women' of the *Notebook* begins with the visit of a teachers' delegation to the Soviet Union. Some of the teachers are pro- and others anti-Stalinist. They enter into fierce debate with one other: 'I was a hundred-percent party member. And there was Harry, a dirty Trot, so there were high words and we parted for ever.'[43] Then we get a taste of the neurotic state of mind concerning sex. Here we cite a few paragraphs from 'A Short Story' (the numbering follows the original):

39   *Ibid.*, xiv.
40   *Ibid.*, 49.
41   *Ibid.*, 279.
42   *Ibid.*, 280.
43   *Ibid.*, 450–1.

no.1.

A woman, starved for love, meets a man rather younger than herself, younger perhaps in emotional experience than in years; or perhaps in the depth of his emotional experience. She deludes herself about the nature of the man; for him, another love affair merely. [...]

no. 2.

A man uses grown-up language, the language of emotionally grown people, to gain a woman. [...].

no. 4.

A healthy woman, in love with a man. She finds herself becoming ill, with symptoms she has never had in her life. She slowly understands that this illness is not hers, she understands the man is ill, She understands the nature of the illness, not from him, how he acts or what he says, but from his illness as reflected in herself. [...]

no. 11.

Two people together, in any kind of relationship – mother, son; father, daughter; lovers; it doesn't matter. One of them acutely neurotic. [...]

no. 12.

A husband, unfaithful to his wife, not because he is in love with another woman, but in order to assert his independence of the married state, comes back from sleeping with the other woman, with every intention of being discreet, but 'accidently' does something to give the show away. This 'accident', scent or lipstick or forgetting to wash off the smell of sex is in fact why he did it in the first place, though he doesn't know it. He needed to say to his wife: I'm not going to belong to you. [...]

no. 15.

An American man, English woman. She, in all her attitudes, emotions, expects to be possessed and taken. He, in all his attitudes and emotions, expects to be taken. Regards himself as an instrument to be used, by her, for her pleasure. Emotional deadlock. Then they discuss it. The discussion, on sexual emotional attitudes turns into a comparison of the two different societies. [...][44]

The Golden Notebook, so it seems, is a treatise on the nature of humankind. It is a study of what, in her Nobel Prize Lecture, Doris Lessing called the 'fragmenting culture' in which our present generation flounders. But have there not been similar conflicts in all generations? The difference now is that we have a writer able to expose this state of social behaviour so openly, and in words never so distinctly expressed before. Yet the *Notebook* is characteristic of modern fiction, with its task of 'constantly amalgamating disparate experience', as T. S. Eliot put it, trying to make sense of the 'chaotic, irregular, fragmentary' experiences of the ordinary person.

Feminist writers have variously read and interpreted Doris Lessing's writings. *The Golden Notebook,* writes Susan Watkins, 'establishes an important distinction between the nostalgic mourning of empire and the melancholy cosmopolitanism of post-national post-war culture [...]'.[45] Diana Wallace maintains that the texts offer 'a highly suggestive exploration of the ageing process and its complex relations with identity, femininity, the body and decay, and objection'.[46] Phyllis Perrakis believes that Doris Lessing has helped to explain 'the spiritual development of the midlife and older woman [...] as a dynamic spiral of consciousness – a movement back that facilitates the move forward, a revisiting of the past enriched by the perspective of the present that leads to a transformative future'.[47] Victoria Rosner argues that 'domestic space in the colonies was inexorably linked to the maternal body, creating the grounds for the psychological and territorial contest of a daughter's separation from her mother'.[48]

Feminist criticism is disposed to proliferate excessively on hidden meanings and motives opened up by Freud. Where the simple facts of life and the weaknesses of human nature ought to be regulated by propriety, diagnosis is sought in psychoanalytic phraseology. They 'always read much

44   *Ibid.,* 455–61.
45   Susan Watkins, *Doris Lessing* (Manchester: Manchester University Press, 2010), 79.
46   Quoted in: *Ibid.,* 172.
47   Quoted in: *Ibid.,* 172.
48   Quoted in: *Ibid.,* 173.

more into this than the writer ever intends,' Doris Lessing herself declared.[49] When she wrote *The Golden Notebook* she was not, she says, 'writing a treatise on feminine stereotypes of the 60s. To the very end, I wanted to tell a story which neither political positions nor sociological analyses were capable of exhausting.'[50] She tried to present 'in a given period of time, the problems that nearly everyone faces at that time'. She did not believe that 'the writer's role should be to forecast, to condemn, to proclaim, etc., or not necessarily. A writer is not a professor. [...] in my case, I never wished to offer a program of ideas or behavior guides. If I had been in possession of such programs I certainly would never have written.'[51] When she began to work on the *The Golden Notebook*, she did not, she says:

> claim absolutely to be doing a thesis on the feminine condition, on the couple, or on the construction of the novel. I was simply trying to understand what was happening to us, to all of us, who refused to live according to 'conventional morality'. And who all encountered, nevertheless, many difficulties, submissive to the point of absurdity in our need to proclaim our freedom. Just like others, moreover, timid conformists, or traditional males, who didn't live very much better than we, they too prey to their inconsistency, their burdensome great principles, their need to distingish themselves.[52]

Doris's works are not necessarily pioneering in portraying the sorry state of women in society. It would be a gross error in thinking to over-stress this, one perhaps sometimes made because of ignorance. Historical literature serves us with richer instances to show women's hopeless position, but also their determination to assert their honour and courage. Antigone bewails:

> Oh, Ismene, Ismene, are we to be spared no punishment from Heaven? Is there any pain or humiliation left for us to suffer? [...][53]

---

49   Doris Lessing, *Conversations*, edited by Earl G. Ingersoll, 191.
50   *Ibid.*, 193.
51   Doris Lessing, Interview with Jean-Maurice de Montremy: 'A Writer Is Not a Professor', in *Ibid.*, 193.
52   *Ibid.*, 198.
53   Sophocles, 'Antigone' in *Four Greek Plays* translated by Kenneth Mcleish (London: Longmans, 1964), 60.

And even when her death is announced, she declares she is prepared to
face it.

> [...]
> Which of the gods have I offended? Which
> Of them laid down the laws that I have broken?
> None! It was Creon I offended: his
> Was the law I dared to break! If he is right,
> It is just for the gods to punish me now,
> And I accept their judgement. [...]⁵⁴

Women do possess wit, perhaps 'not enough wit to keep itself sweet', as
Dr Johnson would imply; but hear Charmian in *Antony and Cleopatra*:

> Good now, some excellent fortune! Let me be married to three kings in a forenoon,
> and widow them all; let me have a child at fifty, to whom Herod of Jewry may do
> homage; find me to marry me with Octavius Caesar, and companion me with my
> mistress.

And what a brave woman Cleopatra was!

> Give me my robe, put on my crown; I have
> Immortal longings in me; now no more
> The juice of Egypt's grape shall moist this lip.
> Yare, yare, good Iras; quick: Methinks I hear
> Antony call; I see him rouse himself
> To praise my noble act; I hear him mock
> The luck of Caesar, which the gods give men
> To excuse their after wrath: husband, I come:
> Now to that name my courage prove my title!
> I am fire and air; my other elements
> I give to baser life. So; have you done? [...]

Jane Eyre displayed strong character in her own way. This was in 1847. She
would not tolerate 'words of love and promise' from Mr Rochester, nor
would she have 'Soft scene, daring demonstration':

54   *Ibid.*, 85.

a weapon of defence must be prepared – I whetted my tongue; as he reached me, I asked with asperity, 'whom he was going to marry now?'

'That was a strange question to be put by his darling Jane'.

'Indeed! I considered it a very natural and necessary one: he had talked of his future wife dying with him. What did he mean by such a pagan idea? *I* had no intention of dying with him – he might depend on that.'[55]

Now these women hardly thought that they were the precursors of the feminist movement, yet nevertheless they demonstrated their strong will. In ages past, women have indeed been denied basic human rights, have been insulted, degraded, and treated as slaves, and it was absolutely indispensable that women liberation movements should struggle so that they could achieve equality with men in every aspect of social life. Not in every country but in most civilized nations, they have advanced a long way in pursuing this aim. Doris Lessing certainly added her voice to enhance the cause of women, although her books were designed to draw our attention to problems between men and women, to 'deal with forces, raveling and unraveling affairs, in which the two sexes do not have the same point of view'.[56]

Doris's non-fiction offers a striking exposure of African society; it is historically veracious. There is in these writings, as George Eliot would say, a 'rare, precious quality of truthfulness'. Her *Going Home* (1957) is a moving and affectionate description of Southern Rhodesia, which she visited after an absence of nearly seven years. It is a personal document, woven into which are 'reminiscences, anecdotes and incidents, both grim and funny'. In *African Laughter* (1992) she recounted her visits to what is now Zimbabwe with equal learning and generosity.

When volume two of Doris's autobiography *Walking in the Shade* appeared, it was widely acclaimed by the critics. There was, we are told, a 'passionate courage spoken by each page of her writing' (Natasha Walter,

---

55   Charlotte Bronte, *Jane Eyre* (London: J. M. Dent & sons Ltd., 1966), 271–2.
56   Lessing, *Conversations*, 194.

Guardian); she was 'a wise and a major figure, a subtle voice' (Malcolm Bradbury, *Observer*); her book was 'a highly idiosyncratic and utterly compelling mixture' (Caroline Moore, *Sunday Telegraph*). Yet the basic facts of her life tell us more: she had to struggle with poverty, with communist intrigues and with personal difficulties. At heart, she was a very emotional person and melancholic. Doris Lessing never wrote great poetry, but what little she wrote reveals this:

> Oh cherry trees, you are too white for my heart,
> And all the ground is whitened with your dying,
> And all your boughs go dipping towards the river,
> And every drop is falling from my heart. [...][57]

Yet melancholy did not diminish her drive and fascination with life, nor was she ever daunted by criticism, although she aroused a good deal of controversy. She employed her time and talent in the most profitable manner open to her – to write great literature. And, if she had an ardent ambition for literary fame, she achieved it during her lifetime. Surely Samuel Johnson would have been disposed to say, 'This woman was fundamentally sensible,' and to quote Virgil: *Non equidem invideo; miror magis*[58] – 'I grudge thee not, rather I marvel.'

---

57   Doris Lessing, 'Oh Cherry Trees You Are Too White' and 'Fable', in *Fourteen Poems* (London: Jonathan Clowes and Scorpion Press, 1959).

58   Virgil, *Eclogues* i. II, in, for instance Loeb Classical Library, *Virgil* vol 1 (Cambridge MA: Harvard University Press, new edition 1999).

Bibliography

1. Archival Sources

The National Archives, Kew, Richmond, Surrey: the British Security Service Personal Files: Communists and Suspected Communists, Including Russian and Communist Sympathisers: *Doris May Lessing*. This material is a Crown Copyright public record, reproduced in this volume under the terms of the *Open Government Licence* (OGL).

Doris May Lessing
Reference:
KV2/4054
KV2/4055
KV2/4056
KV2/4057
KV2/4058

2. Published Works

Blake, Robert, *A History of Rhodesia* (London: Eyre Methuen, 1977).
Andrew, Christopher, *The Defence of the Realm: The Authorized History of MI5* (London: Alan Lane, 2009).
Conrad, Peter, *The Everyman History of English Literature* (London: J.M. Dent & Sons, 1985).
Eaden, James, and David Renton, *The Communist Party of Great Britain Since 1920* (Basingstoke: Palgrave Macmillan, 2002).
Lessing, Doris, *The Grass Is Singing* (London: Michael Joseph, 1950).
——*Martha Quest* (London: Granada Publishing, 1952).

——*A Proper Marriage* (London: Granada Publishing,1954).

——*Going Home*. Drawings by Paul Hogarth (London: Michael Joseph, 1957).

——*A Ripple From The Storm* (London: Granada Publishing, 1958).

——'Oh Cherry Trees You Are Too White For My Heart' and 'Fable', in *Fourteen Poems* (London: Jonathan Clowes and Scorpion Press, 1959).

——*Landlocked* (London: Granada Publishing, 1965).

——*In Pursuit of the English* (MacGibbon and Kee, 1960).

——*The Golden Notebook* (New York: Simon and Schuster, 1962).

——*African Laughter* (London: HarperCollins, 1992).

——*Under My Skin* (London: HarperCollins, 1994).

——*Conversations*, edited by Earl G. Ingersoll (Princeton: Ontario Review Press, 1994).

——*Walking in the Shade* (London: HarperCollins, 1997).

Masterman, J. C., *The Double Cross System in the War of 1939 to 1945* (London: Sphere Books, 1973).

Sinclair, Andrew, *The Red and the Blue: Intelligence, Treason and the Universities* (London: Weidenfeld and Nicolson, 1986).

Watkins, Susan, *Doris Lessing* (Manchester: Manchester University Press, 2010).

Index

By the same author:

Heinrich von Kleist: Poems: Introduced and translated into English rhyming verse
ISBN 978-1-80079-043-8/94 pp./2020
George 'Dadie' Rylands: Shakespearean Scholar and Cambridge Legend
ISBN 978-1-78997-693-9/461 pp./2020
John Sparrow: Warden of All Souls College, Oxford
'I loathe all common things'
ISBN 978-1-78707-506-1 /806 pp./ 2017
The Seventh Earl Beauchamp: A Victim of His Times
ISBN 978-1-906165-62-8 /521 pp./ 2016
House of Lords Reform: A History
   Volume 1. The Origins to 1911: Proposals Deferred
      Book One: The Origins to 1911
      Book Two: 1911–1937
    ISBN 978-3-0343-0749-9 /Book One: 632 pp., Book Two: 633pp./ 2011
   Volume 2. Hopes Rekindled: 1943–1958
    ISBN 978-3-0343-0954-7 / 886 pp./ 2013
   Volume 3. Reforms Attempted: 1960–1969
    ISBN 978-3-0343-1764-1 /956 pp./ 2014
   Volume 4. The Exclusion of Hereditary Peers: 1971–2104
      Book One: 1971–2001
      Book Two: 2001–2014
    ISBN 9783-3-0343-1856-3 / Book One: 632 pp., Book Two: 654 pp./ 2015
A Daring Venture: Rudolf Hess and the Ill-Fated Peace Mission of 1941
ISBN 978-3-0343-1776-4 /278 pp./ 2014
A. V. Dicey: General Characteristics of English Constitutionalism: Six Unpublished Lectures. With a Foreword by Lord Plant of Highfield
ISBN 978-3-03911-955-4 /180 pp./ 2009
Bishop George Bell: House of Lords Speeches and Correspondence with Rudolf Hess
ISBN 978-3-03911-895-3 /241 pp./ 2009
To order, please visit <www.peterlang.com>

PETER LANG
PROMPT

Peter Lang Prompts offer our authors the opportunity to publish original research in small volumes that are shorter and more affordable than traditional academic monographs. With a faster production time, this concise model gives scholars the chance to publish time-sensitive research, open a forum for debate, and make an impact more quickly. Like all Peter Lang publications, Prompts are thoroughly peer reviewed and can even be included in series.

For further information, please contact:

Peter Lang Ltd,
International Academic Publishers,
52 St Giles, Oxford,
OX1 3LU, United Kingdom

To order, please contact our Customer Service Department:

orders@peterlang.com

Visit our website: www.peterlang.com

Prompts include:

Claudia Aburto Guzmán, *Poesía reciente de voces en diálogo con la ascendencia hispano-hablante en los Estados Unidos: Antología breve*. ISBN 978-1-4331-5207-8. 2020

Tywan Ajani, *Barriers to Rebuilding the African American Community: Understanding the Issues Facing Today's African Americans from a Social Work Perspective*. ISBN 978-1-4331-7681-4. 2020

Marcilio de Freitas and Marilene Corrêa da Silva Freitas, *The Future of Amazonia in Brazil: A Worldwide Tragedy*. ISBN 978-1-4331-7793-4. 2020

Janet Farrell Leontiou, *The Doctor Still Knows Best: How Medical Culture Is Still Marked by Paternalism*. Health Communication, vol. 15. ISBN 978-1-4331-7322-6. 2020

Clare Gorman (ed.), *Miss-representation: Women, Literature, Sex and Culture*. ISBN 978-1-78874-586-4. 2020

Eva Marín Hlynsdóttir. *Gender in Organizations: The Icelandic Female Council Manager*. ISBN 978-1-4331-7729-3. 2020

Micol Kates, *Towards a Vegan-Based Ethic: Dismantling Neo-Colonial Hierarchy Through an Ethic of Lovingkindness*. ISBN 978-1-4331-7797-2. 2020

Josiane Ranguin, *Mediating the Windrush Children: Caryl Phillips and Horace Ové*. ISBN 978-1-4331-7424-7. 2020

Dylan Scudder, *Coffee and Conflict in Colombia: Part of the Pentalemma Series on Managing Global Dilemmas*. ISBN 978-1-4331-7568-8. 2020

Dylan Scudder, *Conflict Minerals in the Democratic Republic of Congo: Part of the Pentalemma Series on Managing Global Dilemmas*. ISBN 978-1-4331-7561-9. 2020

Dylan Scudder, *Mining Conflict in the Philippines: Part of the Pentalemma Series on Managing Global Dilemmas*. ISBN 978-1-4331-7632-6. 2020

Dylan Scudder, *Multi-Hazard Disaster in Japan: Part of the Pentalemma Series on Managing Global Dilemmas*. ISBN 978-1-4331-7530-5. 2020

Shai Tubali, *Cosmos and Camus: Science Fiction Film and the Absurd*. ISBN 978-1-78997-664-9. 2020

Angela Williams, *Hip Hop Harem: Women, Rap and Representation in the Middle East*. ISBN 978-1-4331-7295-3. 2020

Ivan Zhavoronkov (trans.), *The Socio-Cultural and Philosophical Origins of Science* by Anatoly Nazirov. ISBN 978-1-4331-7228-1. 2020

Peter Raina, *Heinrich von Kleist Poems*. ISBN 978-1-80079-043-8. 2020

Geanneti Tavares Salomon, *Fashion and Irony in* Dom Casmurro. ISBN 978-1-78997-972-5. 2021

Peter Raina, *Doris Lessing: A Life Behind the Scenes*. ISBN 978-1-80079-183-1. 2021

Printed by
CPI books GmbH, Leck